FRESH POWER

Resources by Jim Cymbala

Fresh Wind, Fresh Fire
(book and audio)

Fresh Faith
(book and audio)

Fresh Power
(book and audio)

The Life God Blesses
(book and audio)

The Church God Blesses
(book and audio)

Breakthrough Prayer
(book and audio)

When God's People Pray
(curriculum)

FRESH POWER

What Happens When
God Leads
And You Follow

JIM CYMBALA
WITH DEAN MERRILL

ZONDERVAN®

ZONDERVAN.com/
AUTHORTRACKER
follow your favorite authors

We want to hear from you. Please send your comments about this book to us in care of zreview@zondervan.com. Thank you.

Fresh Power
Copyright © 2001 by Jim Cymbala
Study Guide Copyright © 2003 by Jim Cymbala

This title is also available as a Zondervan audio product.

Requests for information should be addressed to:

Zondervan, *Grand Rapids, Michigan 49530*

The Library of Congress has catalogued the original hardcover edition as follows:

Cymbala, Jim, 1943–
    Fresh power: experiencing the vast resources of the spirit of God / Jim Cymbala
with Dean Merrill.
       p.   cm.
    Includes bibliographical references.
    ISBN-10: 0-310-23008-X (hardcover)
    ISBN-13: 978-0-310-23008-3 (hardcover)
    1. Holy Spirit. I. Title.
BT121.2.C96 2001
231'.3—dc21
                                        00-049993

ISBN-10: 0-310-25154-0 (softcover)
ISBN-13: 978-0-310-25154-5 (softcover)

All Scripture quotations, unless otherwise indicated, are taken from the *Holy Bible: New International Version*®. NIV®. Copyright © 1973, 1978, 1984 by International Bible Society. Used by permission of Zondervan. All rights reserved. Italics used in quotations from Scripture have been inserted by the author.

Interior design by Rob Monacelli

Printed in the United States of America

---

12 13 • 27 26 25 24 23 22 21 20 19 18

CONTENTS

PROLOGUE

BY D. L. MOODY

TOWARD THE END OF *the nineteenth century, the greatest Christian evangelist alive at that time called a special convocation. D. L. Moody summoned people to his hometown of Northfield, Massachusetts, "for prayer and waiting upon the Lord for a new enduement of power from on high." Moody, who had started out his working life in the shoe business, had never received ordination but nevertheless was greatly used of God both in America and across Great Britain, seeing hundreds of thousands come to Christ. He became a household name among believers everywhere. He was known and appreciated as a careful student of the Bible, staying humble amid his great popularity.*

But Mr. Moody's heart became increasingly concerned over the years as he saw spiritual decline in so many churches. How could he, as an evangelist, effectively extend God's kingdom if the local congregations were lukewarm? Where would converts go to be fed and nurtured?

In response to Moody's appeal, hundreds came from nearly every state and several foreign countries for the meetings conducted during this special convocation. His talks were condensed into a book published a few months later under the title Secret Power.[1] *It began as follows:*

There has been much inquiry of late on the Holy Spirit. In this and other lands, thousands of persons have been giving attention to the study of this grand theme. I hope it will lead us all to pray for a greater manifestation of His power upon the whole church of God.

How much we have dishonored Him in the past! How ignorant of His grace and love and presence we have been! True, we have heard of Him and read of Him, but we have had little intelligent knowledge of His attributes, His offices, and His relations to us. . . .

Let others reject, if they will, at their own peril, this imperishable truth. I believe, and am growing more into this belief, that divine, miraculous, creative power resides in the Holy Spirit. . . .

Unless He attend the word in power, vain will be the attempt in preaching it. Human eloquence or persuasiveness of speech are the mere trappings of the dead. If the living Spirit be absent, the prophet may preach to the bones in the valley, but it must be the breath from heaven that will cause the slain to live. . . .

If we want that power to quicken our friends who are dead in sin, we must look to God, and not be looking to man to do it. If we look alone to ministers, if we look alone to Christ's disciples to do this work, we shall be disappointed. If we look to the Spirit of God and expect it to come from Him and Him alone, then we shall honor the Spirit, and the Spirit will do His work.

I cannot help but believe that there are many Christians who want to be more efficient in the Lord's service. It is from the Holy Spirit that we may expect this power.

ONE

A Long Night in Indianapolis

In the fall of 1994 I was invited to speak at a Christian music gathering in Indianapolis. I had visited once before, so I knew that some 10,000 people came mainly to hear great gospel singing. Yes, there was a speaker each morning and also a number of workshops throughout the day, but the drawing card of the event was the musical praise and worship.

I arrived on a Thursday, and that evening I still wasn't sure what I should speak about the next morning. I was leaning toward a simple message of encouragement—one I had preached before. I thought it would go well in this festive setting. I certainly didn't want to do anything controversial or get in anybody's face about anything. On this, my first chance to speak to this large gathering, my human nature wanted to be liked and accepted.

I went to part of the evening concert with my daughter and son-in-law, Chrissy and Al Toledo, but left around eight o'clock to return to my hotel room. There I began to seek the Lord about my message for the next morning. I knew that out of the thousands of good Bible verses a preacher could profitably use, there must be one passage that the Lord specifically had in mind for that occasion and that audience.

Over the years I've tried to pray along these lines before speaking, asking God not only for his anointing but also for a confirmation of the subject for each occasion.

I reviewed my sermon outline and then went to prayer. After all, I knew I needed his help for this message to prove a blessing to the people.

OFF TRACK

The longer I prayed, the more this nice, familiar sermon idea went dead inside of me. There was no stirring in my heart. The outline was biblical enough, to be sure, and no doubt the people would be helped by it. But I knew it wasn't the right fit. Something else was waiting in the wings for me. And to be honest, I didn't really want to find out what it was.

I kept praying. In time I felt drawn toward the text "My house will be called a house of prayer" (Mark 11:17), a message I had preached not long before at the Brooklyn Tabernacle. It's a very direct message. It deals with Jesus' cleaning the merchants out of the temple and pointedly calls the audience to what the church is really for, as opposed to all the misuses we make of it. (This message later became part of my first book as a chapter entitled "The Day Jesus Got Mad.")

> I began to argue with the Lord. A sermon on cleaning merchants out of the house of God—at a music festival? Surely not!

I began to argue with the Lord. A sermon on cleaning merchants out of the house of God—at a music festival? Surely not! "God, I'm not a regular speaker at this gathering. I have no right to stand up and confront these people. They'll be sitting there thinking, *Who does he think he is—some New York City wise guy? This is starting to sound like a revival service.*

They didn't invite me here to stir up controversy. If I tell them that today's church has become prayerless and is in danger of Jesus coming in judgment . . . well, this is hardly the way to win friends and influence people."

It was getting late. I had no notes for that message anyway. I could remember only parts and pieces of what I had preached at home. Surely I wasn't going to get up in front of 10,000 people and just "wing it."

Yet the Holy Spirit seemed to persistently whisper to my heart, *This is why I brought you here. This is what I want you to preach. Are you going to do my will, or are you just going to go out there tomorrow morning and "perform"?*

I kept struggling in prayer. This whole situation was getting messy. If I didn't get my act together soon and get some sleep, I was headed for a big embarrassment. Why couldn't I just follow through on what I had planned?

On the other hand, if I went against what God wanted me to do, I would fail the Lord who called me into the ministry.

Finally, after an hour or two, I relented. I opened my Bible to the passage in Mark as I said, "God, help me. If you want to use this to speak to the people tomorrow morning, all right. Show me how to reconstruct this sermon."

Around midnight something very unusual happened. I'm normally not a timid person, but on this night I was attacked by a tremendous feeling of fear and insecurity. I began to imagine the audience turning against me. Something or someone kept whispering to me that this "prophetic" message wasn't going to fit the setting at all. It seemed as if I was battling against forces intent on disrupting this message I now felt so strongly.

My heart began to pound. I started pacing around the room. Before long, I was crying. "O God, now that you've shown me your will, and I'm willing to do it—give me the courage, the power, the wisdom to preach this message for your glory."

I turned out the light and tried to get some sleep, but couldn't. Soon I was back up again, pacing and praying. I kept battling an ominous sense that this whole thing was going to be a disaster. Finally, around three-thirty I fell asleep out of sheer exhaustion.

The sun had just come up that Friday morning when the telephone rang. It wasn't my wake-up call from the hotel desk; it was my wife, Carol, back in New York. "Jim, are you okay?" she asked with a worried tone.

"Yes, I think so," I answered groggily.

"What's going on there with you?" she persisted.

"Well, the truth is, I'm in a battle," I admitted. "I have to speak in a couple of hours, and the Lord's been dealing with me about a message that's not easy to preach. I'm really struggling."

"I knew something was wrong," she replied. "I couldn't sleep last night. I woke up and had to intercede for you. I didn't know what was going on, but somehow I was really burdened for you." She then began praying for me right there on the phone.

When she finished, she added, "God's going to help you, Jim. Just depend on the Holy Spirit to help you, and let it go."

INTO THE ARENA

I hung up the phone and, on less than four hours' sleep, began getting ready for the day ahead. All too soon I was across the street at the arena. The sound of all the people singing at the start of the morning session echoed through the corridors.

Someone came to put the clip-on microphone on my tie. That was my first signal that I wouldn't have the usual hand-held mike, which is what I'm most comfortable with when I speak because it gives me something to do with one hand. Worse than that—the audiovisual technician reminded me that I would be on a center stage in the round, with people on all sides, which meant I would have to remember to keep turning continually to face new sections, one after another. And a set of video cameras would be following me!

From my point of view, the circumstances could not have been more awkward.

As the host began to introduce me, I walked out onto the circle stage and nervously took stock of what I was up against. *O God, help me now!* I prayed silently.

I began speaking in a soft voice. "I want to talk for a few moments about something so vital, and yet it's so simple. It's so familiar to us—and that's the danger. I want our session this morning to be something that will make a difference in our lives. . . .

"To approach this subject, I want to give you one of the most strange and stunning pictures of Jesus found anywhere in the Bible." I then began to describe Jesus' cleansing of the temple.

It seemed that the longer I spoke, the more clarity came into my heart. I felt calm inside. I could sense the Holy Spirit helping me. I kept walking and turning as I spoke, looking out into the sea of faces that stretched upward into shadows on all sides. Without notes, the logic and sequence of my remarks seemed to fall together. Even though I was saying some difficult things for people to hear—that gospel music had the potential to be mere entertainment rather than genuine ministry, for example—they seemed to respond. Their hearts were engaged.

My tone was not harsh or condescending. Instead, I expressed the cry of my own heart for more of God. The burden within me was transferred to those who listened. In time I came to feel almost removed from what was taking place. It was as if I was lifted up and watching the stage from one of the upper seats. All nervousness and self-consciousness were gone now. I was just pouring out what I felt God wanted me to say.

As I came to the end, I told the story of how desperate prayer had pulled our teenage daughter Chrissy back from rebellion and self-destruction to serve the Lord again. (In fact, Chrissy and her husband were now sitting there in the audience listening to me.) Some of the last sentences I uttered were, "God says that when you call, he will answer. The hard cases some of you are facing today—the answer won't come from another seminar.... We have too many mere technicians who are only stressing methodology, and they are increasingly invading the church. The answer is not in any human methodology. The answer is in the power of the Holy Spirit. The answer is in the grace of God." I then did something unusual for that type of gathering: I made a direct call for response.

> We have too many mere technicians who are only stressing methodology, and they are increasingly invading the church. The answer is not in any human methodology.

There was very little area to use around the stage, so I simply had people stand who wanted to call upon God in prayer for situations that only God could help. Possibly they had given up because it seemed so hopeless: wayward children, spiritual weakness, marriages under siege. A number of them edged toward the center anyway and began to call upon the Lord, many with tears. "O God, intervene in my life and the crisis I'm facing," they prayed. "Have mercy upon us and stretch out your hand of power as you promised to do."

I walked off the stage, removed my tie-clip microphone, and was soon ushered to a car to return to the Indianapolis airport. Some of the folks shook my hand and thanked me. Inside, I felt peace: God had indeed helped me do what he wanted in that place.

RIPPLES IN THE WATER

During the next few months I chatted occasionally with my friend who had invited me, and he mentioned that sales of that morning's video were beyond any in their previous experience. A year later, even after two or three years, the video continued to sell and to spread all across the country by word of mouth.

Reports came of ministerial groups watching it in far-away places. Faxes and e-mails continually arrived. A conference of more than 2,000 people in New England watched it during a main session, and when the tape ended, a prayer meeting broke out as people spontaneously went to the throne of grace.

More than one pastor called to say, "I don't know you personally, but I just wanted you to know that I showed your video in my first morning service—and the people got up en masse to come pray at the altar, which is not the custom in our church. When it was time for them to clear out so the next crowd could come in for the next service, I didn't know what to do. . . . The new people just came in and joined the first group in calling upon God and waiting in his presence."

A godly revival ministry in Michigan was blessed by a donor who paid for thousands of copies to go to spiritually hungry pastors. Great reports kept coming back of what transpired—*all because the Lord took over my plans in a hotel room and showed me his will.* I hadn't wanted to preach that message at all. But God knew exactly why he had me there.

When I think back to that long night in Indianapolis, I think about Jesus' words in John 16:7: "I tell you the truth: It is for your good that I am going away. Unless I go away, the Counselor will not come to you; but if I go, I will send him to you."

This must have sounded very strange to the disciples. They had been at Jesus' side for more than three years; he was everything to them. They moved when he moved. He answered all their questions. When they were sad or apprehensive, he assured them. It was unthinkable that Jesus should ever leave them, or that this would be a *good* or even *better* thing.

But our Lord knew what was best. His statement highlighted the greatness of the Holy Spirit's coming ministry in their lives and the life of the Christian church. The Holy Spirit would be everything to them, even more than the physical Jesus had been. They would accomplish more under his direction and power than they had ever done in the time of Jesus. That is not blasphemous or degrading to Christ, because he said it himself.

Jesus had been with them, but he was *outside of them*. And the great work that needed to be done in the disciples was internal. This was at the very heart of the New Covenant that God was making with his people: "I will give you a new heart and put a new spirit in you; I will remove from you your heart of stone and give you a heart of flesh. And I will put my Spirit in you" (Ezekiel 36:26–27).

While Christ's work on the cross, the shedding of his blood, was the only way to settle the problem of guilt, sin, and condemnation, the coming of the promised Holy Spirit was God's way of changing human beings from the inside out. The law given to Moses had failed on this very point. It was in itself holy and just, but the problem was the sinful nature within people. Now the Holy Spirit dwelling in the hearts of believers would conquer the age-old dilemma of "I want to be different but can't. I know what's wrong—but I keep doing it anyway." This empowerment by the Spirit would be the dynamic source throughout time for all who live and labor for Jesus Christ.

OUR EARNEST NEED

What happened to me in Indianapolis was not unusual. It was merely the Holy Spirit coming to the aid of a human vessel who didn't really know what he was supposed to be doing. The Spirit is the one who leads us into God's will. As Jesus had led and inspired his disciples while on earth, the Holy Spirit came to do the same in a more powerful, intimate way.

That night in the hotel room was a case of Romans 8:26, which boldly declares, "The Spirit helps us in our weakness. We do not know what we ought to pray for, but the Spirit himself intercedes for us with groans that words cannot express."

Today this is one of the most neglected truths in the whole New Testament. We Christians seldom admit that we don't know how to pray. Many of us have been taught since childhood how to put sentences together that sound like a prayer, to the point that we are professionals at it. Some can turn out an eloquent presentation to God at a moment's notice.

Prayer born of the Spirit, however, is another dimension of calling on God to the point of having the Holy Spirit supernaturally assist us. This is not a worked-up emotionalism but a powerful promise of help from God himself! The Holy Spirit helped me to pray as I struggled in weakness that night.

The alarm that went off in Carol's heart to pray for me was also a supernatural assistance from the Holy Spirit. He is able to communicate knowledge through other than the natural senses. Carol knew I needed prayer and intercession even though no one had told her of my dilemma—no one, that is, but the omniscient Spirit of God. So she lifted up fervent petitions, going far beyond any mechanical, routine prayer.

The boldness that I needed to go beyond myself in a very intimidating situation came only through the Holy Spirit. He lifted me above my natural fears and verbal limitations. I'm no natural orator, let me assure you. Only the enablement of the Spirit made those words come across with clarity and impact. But this is the very reason that the Spirit has come: to inspire and equip ordinary people to work for Jesus Christ.

> **"The philosophies of men fail, but the Word of God *in the demonstration of the Spirit* prevails."**
> **—Samuel Chadwick**

Almost a hundred years ago in England, a Methodist leader and college president named Samuel Chadwick wrote:

> The work of God is not by might of men or by the power of men but by his Spirit. It is by him the truth convicts and converts, sanctifies and saves. The philosophies of men fail, but the Word of God *in the demonstration of the Spirit* prevails. Our wants are many, and our faults innumerable, but they are all comprehended in our lack of the Holy Ghost. We want nothing but the fire.
>
> The resources of the church are in "the supply of the Spirit." The Spirit is more than the minister of consolation. He is Christ without the limitations of the flesh and the material world. He can reveal what Christ could not speak. He has resources of power greater than those Christ could use, and he makes possible greater works than his. He is the Spirit of God,

the Spirit of truth, the Spirit of witness, the Spirit of conviction, the Spirit of power, the Spirit of holiness, the Spirit of light, the Spirit of adoption, the Spirit of help, the Spirit of liberty, the Spirit of wisdom, the Spirit of revelation, the Spirit of promise, the Spirit of love, the Spirit of meekness, the Spirit of sound mind, the Spirit of grace, the Spirit of glory, and the Spirit of prophecy. It is for the church to explore the resources of the Spirit; the resources of the world are futile.[1]

This "supply of the Spirit" (Philippians 1:19 KJV) is the great need of our hour. We are currently living in the era of the Holy Spirit as we await the return of our Savior Jesus Christ. Our Lord is seated at the Father's right hand in heaven, but he has sent the promised Spirit so that, through his power, we can fulfill all of God's will, defeat every device of Satan, and extend the kingdom of Christ here on earth.

No matter what difficulties confront us as believers or as local congregations, God is calling us to receive today this great promise of power as a living reality. Then in victory we will praise God alongside those believers down through the ages who have experienced for themselves the truth that "greater is he that is in you, than he that is in the world" (1 John 4:4 KJV).

TWO

Of Cemeteries and Insane Asylums

As WE ENTER A new millennium, it is vital for us to take a new, unbiased, teachable look at what exactly God intended for the Christian church. All the frightening prophecies and predictions of Y2K catastrophes are now behind us. We continue to gather as the church of Jesus Christ, and our prayer is to see his kingdom come and his will be done. But this thing we call "church," which we all love and are part of— what was it meant to be?

The world we live in is, of course, antagonistic to our beliefs about Jesus Christ. Our Christian values are rejected out of hand. But instead of engaging this world and proclaiming the gospel of God's love with an accompanying manifestation of God's power, as we find in the Bible, the church is reacting in one of three ways:

1. Running away from the world, circling our wagons, and saying, "Isn't it horrible the way people are living out there?" While it might be true that the world is careening out of moral control, this misses the point concerning our calling to be salt and light.

2. Making harsh and condemning statements about the world and its people, forgetting that they are not our enemy but rather our mission field. This kind of attitude has formed a whole Christian industry, with radio commentators, editorial writers, and others relentlessly attacking and analyzing sinners in both high and low places. But this is not the task of Christians; as Paul (an apostle no less) clearly wrote, "What business is it of mine to judge those outside the church? Are you not to judge those inside? God will judge those outside" (1 Corinthians 5:12–13). Our job is not to castigate unbelievers but rather to humbly look within our own ranks to see if we church people are actually living out the Christian life as God intended.

It is vital to remember that the sternest words of warning and correction found in the New Testament are directed not to the unbelieving masses but rather to Christ's own church. Although God's nature is love, it is a love that calls for caution and, yes, even a holy fear, using the strongest possible terms. Listen to a few sound bites from the inspired Scripture as they address problems found not in the world but among the Lord's people. We are not used to hearing such bold language.

> Brothers, I could not address you as spiritual but as worldly—mere infants in Christ. I gave you milk, not solid food, for you were not yet ready for it. Indeed, you are still not ready. You are still worldly. For since there is jealousy and quarreling among you, are you not worldly? Are you not acting like mere men? (1 Corinthians 3:1–3).

> You cannot drink the cup of the Lord and the cup of demons too; you cannot have a part in both the Lord's table and the table of demons. Are we trying to arouse the Lord's jealousy? Are we stronger than he? (1 Corinthians 10:21–22).

See to it, brothers, that none of you has a sinful, unbelieving heart that turns away from the living God. But
encourage one another daily, as long as it is called
Today, so that none of you may be hardened by sin's
deceitfulness (Hebrews 3:12–13).

I know your deeds, that you are neither cold nor hot.
I wish you were either one or the other! So, because
you are lukewarm—neither hot nor cold—I am about
to spit you out of my mouth (Revelation 3:15–16).

Notice the unequivocal terms God uses to warn his people
about the danger of hearts turning "away from the living God."
The problem here was not secular humanism, moral relativism,
or witchcraft in the Roman Empire. It was the saints of the
Most High drifting away from their high and holy calling.

3. Letting the world "evangelize" us without our realizing it.
George Barna, well-known Christian researcher, reports that
regular churchgoers are shockingly similar to the populace at
large in any number of ways:

- Those who bought a lottery ticket in the past week:
  non-Christians 27%, Christians 23%
- Those who watched a PG–13 or R-rated movie in the
  past three months: non-Christians 87%, Christians
  76%
- Those who have been divorced: non-Christians 23%,
  Christians 27%[1]

Instead of being a holy, powerful remnant that is conse-
crated and available to God (in the New Testament sense of
those words), the world's value system has invaded the church
so that there's almost no distinction between the two.

Wouldn't it be wise to ask ourselves what kind of teaching has brought about this sad state of affairs? What are we

doing, or not doing, that causes such a breakdown in the spiritual fiber of professing Christians? We had better start asking some hard questions and be prepared to throw overboard whatever has made the church so weak and carnal.

Instead of that, a massive cover-up is going on. Rather than face the obvious facts around us, certain church leaders proclaim that everything is fine because they have a "new vision for the church." I hear this in pastors' conferences all over: "What's your vision for your church?" If you don't have a fancy-sounding new concept all memorized to recite, you're behind the times.

But how can that be? The Brooklyn Tabernacle is not *my* church; it's God's. He is the vision-setter, not me. Jesus Christ is the Head, and we are his Body. In the Bible he gave us *his* vision for the church—what it is supposed to be, how it is supposed to operate, what its goals are, what power will sustain its working. To hold any vision apart from Christ's vision as stated in the Bible is the height of arrogance. It will also be spiritually fatal.

> The Brooklyn Tabernacle is not *my* church; it's God's. He is the vision-setter, not me.

For example, think of all the church-growth experts whose vision for the modern, "cutting-edge" church includes everything but prayer. The prayer meeting, which was the engine that drove the apostolic church, is found nowhere in their new vision. To them, the Bible is a dated book. Prayer and the power of God's Spirit are seldom mentioned in their slick journals. Meanwhile, their human cleverness produces only insipid little meetings that fail to connect people with God ... few if any testimonies of unbelievers being radically changed by the power of the gospel ... little confrontation of sin ... no disciplining of those within the church who violate the Christian rule of conduct.

What if, in the end, the local church turns out to be little more than a glorified entertainment center with no resemblance to the models given us in holy Scripture?

If we pastors need a vision statement, I have a suggestion: How about the epistles of 1 and 2 Timothy? How about Paul's letter to Titus? How about the book of Acts? These clearly outline what God intended his church to be. If the spirit of our churches bears no resemblance to those in God's Word, then we had better humble ourselves and admit it.

Yes, times do change, and we have access to many advantages, such as buildings of our own, sound systems, and gospel albums. These are all great. But no one has a right to change the abiding spiritual principles of the church laid down by Jesus Christ, who gave his own life on the cross to bring it into being.

THE SPIRIT IS ESSENTIAL

The key to all of this is the person and work of the Holy Spirit. Christianity is hopeless without him. The church cannot be the church without the Holy Spirit abiding and empowering it. The degree to which we understand *and* experience the Spirit of God will be the exact degree to which God's plan for our churches will be accomplished.

If we downgrade the Holy Spirit—worse yet, if we ignore him . . . and even worse than that, if we grieve or quench him—we end up with a modern church that is totally foreign to the New Testament. Church services today in many places have become totally predictable, timed to the minute, devoid of any spontaneity, and with little or no sense of the Spirit's presence. I am afraid the early Christians in the book of Acts would be stunned to see what we now call the church of Jesus Christ. But we're so used to it after all these years that it sadly seems normal to us.

Godly, spiritual men saw this danger hundreds of years ago. Listen to the words of William Law, the English devotional author and contemporary of John Wesley, in 1761:

> Where the Holy Spirit is not honored as *the one through whom the whole life and power of gospel salvation is to be effected*, it is no wonder that Christians have no more of the reality of the gospel than the Jews had of the purity of the Law.... For the New Testament without the coming of the Holy Spirit in power over self, sin, and the devil is no better a help to heaven than the Old Testament without the coming of the Messiah.[2]

> Thousands stand ready to split doctrinal hairs and instruct others in the fine meaning of Scripture words— but there are *so few through whom the Holy Spirit can work to bring men to new birth in the kingdom of God.*[3]

> The Pharisee rested so thoroughly in the law, that he rejected the Saviour to whom the law directed him. The sound evangelical thinks that when he has mastered the letter of the gospel, he thereby knows its truth and power. And thus, while claiming allegiance to Paul's doctrine, *he knows little of Paul's spiritual experience* which caused him to say, "I can do all things through Christ who strengthens me."[4]

Reread those words, and think what a burning challenge they are to us today. The very people who are thumping the Bible the most vigorously are often the ones trying to have a church without the Holy Spirit. They think that teaching alone can cause their members to live a "victorious Christian life"— but it can't be done without experiencing the power of the Holy Spirit. Vows and promises alone, no matter how sincere, can never overcome the power of the world, the flesh, and the devil.

How many people today casually dismiss the Bible's clear record of the Holy Spirit's power and working—with no verses to support their opinion? I know that Old Testament restrictions about eating pork or wearing clothing of mixed fabric were overruled by clear New Testament teaching. But there are *no* New Testament verses that tell us to dismiss the precedent of the Holy Spirit's activity in Acts. Nothing in the writings of Paul or Peter or John or Jude says, "Oh, by the way—what the Spirit accomplished through simple, untrained men in the early church can never happen again. Just forget it and try your best with eloquent sermons and clever human programs." Jesus Christ is the same yesterday, today, and forever, and so is the Holy Spirit.

> **Vows and promises alone, no matter how sincere, can never overcome the power of the world, the flesh, and the devil.**

Martyn Lloyd-Jones, a well-known British preacher of the twentieth century, wrote, "The Scriptures never anywhere say that these things were only temporary—never! There is no such statement anywhere.... To hold such a view is simply to quench the Spirit."[5] In a nearby section of the same book this leading evangelical added: "I believe we are in urgent need of some manifestation, some demonstration, of the power of the *Holy Spirit.*"[6]

Are we going to accept the whole Bible concerning God's promises to us, or just part of it?

ON THE OTHER HAND . . .

While some churches such as I have been describing might be referred to as cemeteries ... others on the other side of the spectrum are more like insane asylums. We have some horrendous abuses going on in the name of the Spirit of God. Many in the so-called charismatic movement have done bizarre things that are not only outside New Testament teaching but actually contradict it. When people bark like dogs, laugh like hyenas, roar like lions, and chirp like birds "in the Spirit," someone needs to lift a voice and say, "Where is this found in the Bible? And how does it edify a congregation?"

The New Testament lays down as a first principle that "the manifestation of the Spirit is given for the common good" (1 Corinthians 12:7). For example, the apostle Paul clearly stated that any public speaking in tongues must be followed by interpretation in the common language so that the entire church could understand and be edified. Otherwise, no tongues speaking was allowed, since it was not intelligible to the audience.

If Paul objected to uninterpreted tongues, what would he say about continual flopping, twitching, or spinning like a top? Can anyone imagine Peter, James, or John participating in such madness? Paul's passion for evangelism made him all the more concerned for what "an unbeliever or someone who does not understand" (1 Corinthians 14:24) would think. To Paul, church was definitely not a circus.

How would the apostle react to the videotape I saw of two well-known preachers in a meeting carrying on an apparent comedy routine in other tongues! One man would speak for twenty seconds or so, then the other would suddenly break up laughing. Then he would begin to speak as if trying to "top" the first man's story. Both would then collapse in knee-slapping guffaws. There was no interpretation into English whatsoever. The crowd roared and cheered as if at a carnival. What an unbiblical travesty and insult to the Spirit of God!

Some people, I am afraid, aren't about to submit to the authority of Scripture. They are totally consumed with the latest trendy manifestations and strange new signs that convince them "the river is flowing." If someone were to say, "Excuse me, but that's against the Bible," the person would be dismissed by the familiar reply of "Oh, but God's doing a new thing, brother!"

My pastor friends in Argentina tell me that North American evangelists have come their way preaching that if you really have a childlike attitude toward the things of God, you will evidence the behavior of children. How? By "drooling in the Spirit." Such insanity is an embarrassment to all thinking Christians.

Does God do things so new that they are not in the Bible? If the Scriptures are not the judge of supposed "Holy Spirit manifestations," where will this all end? What if someone came up with a prophecy that said, "Thus saith the Lord: Why are you worshiping only me, and not my chief angel Gabriel? He has been ignored for far too long. I am deeply offended over this. You must change your ways."

The rebuttal of "Wait a minute—that's not in the Bible" would have no clout, would it? The other person could always say, "Don't you know, God's doing a new thing!"

That kind of fanaticism would never have made it in the book of Acts. When, as we read in chapter 2, the apostle Peter stood up to explain the remarkable goings-on on the Day of Pentecost, he spent nearly half his message quoting the Old Testament. When, a number of years later in Acts 17, an evangelistic team rolled into Berea and started proclaiming new things, the local residents "examined the Scriptures every day to see if what Paul said was true" (v. 11). They didn't seem to focus on whether they felt "blessed" or not. They didn't take an opinion poll. They didn't even look at the crowd size as a measure of endorsement. They instead went straight to the plumb line of the eternal Word of God.

In 1 Corinthians 4:6 Paul declares, "Do not go beyond what is written." While we often lament liberal churches that take away from God's Word, we must also beware of those who do the opposite. It is an offense to God when someone attempts to add to Scripture. We have no right to go beyond the book that the Holy Spirit inspired. It is the circumference of our spiritual circle. The Spirit of God will never contradict himself. When we test everything by the Word of God, we are doing nothing more or less than honoring again the Holy Spirit who authored it.

> **We have no right to go beyond the book that the Holy Spirit inspired. It is the circumference of our spiritual circle.**

HOW IT ALL BEGAN

Here is the simple New Testament truth about how the Christian church was born:

In Acts 1, the risen Jesus has appeared to the disciples on and off for forty days. These are the same men who had failed miserably when the pressure came during his arrest. Far more than just doubting Jesus, they turned tail and fled. Peter was worse than that; he verbally denied that he knew Jesus, to the point of cursing.

Yet Jesus is going to entrust these very men with the leadership of the newborn church of Christ, which is his Body!

The world, lying in spiritual darkness, desperately needs the gospel that has just been completed with the sacrificial death and powerful resurrection of Jesus. The disciples are putting it all together in their minds: why Jesus had to die, what it means for humanity, the great task that lies ahead. The Old Testament Scriptures are coming alive right and left for them. The glorified Christ, with fresh nail prints still in his hands, is tutoring them day after day.

You would think that as Ascension Day draws closer and closer, Jesus would be saying, "Get ready, men, to launch a major campaign. Reserve the Jerusalem Arena for a series of mass meetings. Start the advance publicity. Indeed, maybe you should divide up into teams and hit several cities of Israel at once for maximum effect. The message of redemption through my death on the cross needs to go out far and wide—immediately!"

In actuality, he tells them the opposite.

> On one occasion, while he was eating with them, he gave them this command: "Do not leave Jerusalem, but wait for the gift my Father promised, which you have heard me speak about. For John baptized with water, but in a few days you will be baptized with the Holy Spirit."
>
> So when they met together, they asked him, "Lord, are you at this time going to restore the kingdom to Israel?"
>
> He said to them: "It is not for you to know the times or dates the Father has set by his own authority. But you *will receive power when the Holy Spirit comes on you;* and you will be my witnesses in Jerusalem, and in all Judea and Samaria, and to the ends of the earth."
>
> After he said this, he was taken up before their very eyes, and a cloud hid him from their sight (Acts 1:4–9).

The world is dying; people are without the gospel; these men have the message of life; they have seen Jesus in the flesh and walked with him for days on end, both before and after his death and resurrection—and yet he tells them to wait. Why?

Christ knows the power and strongholds of the enemy. He knows what these men will soon face. He knows how much wisdom, discernment, and boldness they will need. And so he says, "No, even though you have the correct message, you will never accomplish the task I give you without the *power* [Greek: *dunamis*, from which we get the word *dynamite*] of the Holy Spirit, which is greater than yourselves. It will be *his* supernatural ability working in and through you. Don't go anywhere until you have received that power."

This is truly amazing. It is the opposite of what we hear in our day: "Just get a good theological education, and then go out to preach the message you've learned in the classroom." But we are finding in churches all across the country that preaching alone does not cause conversions, does not result in baptisms, and does not expand the kingdom of God. Most churches are making no dent in the masses of unbelievers all around them.

We can blame tough neighborhoods, New Age thinking, and immoral entertainment all we want. But when has the environment *not* been difficult for the gospel? Think of what the early church faced in hostile Jerusalem and the pagan Roman Empire. Yet they received power from on high and did exploits for God instead of just talking to themselves. Their preaching and witnessing had a dimension of supernatural ability that we are sadly lacking today.

Now a lot of us type A personalities don't want to hear the instruction "Wait." We are eager to get going. But we will accomplish far more if we spend time waiting for the power of the Spirit. The work of the church needs not just the correct message concerning Jesus but also the power that Jesus promised his followers.

> A lot of us type A personalities don't want to hear the instruction "Wait." … But we will accomplish far more if we spend time waiting for the power of the Spirit.

Notice that Jesus did not say to wait for any certain manifestation: the flickering flames, the rushing wind, or the speaking in tongues. He pointed them to their need of receiving spiritual *power*. The thrust in the New Testament was always toward the power itself rather than any particular manifestations that came alongside the power. Today I am afraid that this priority sequence is reversed in some circles. People are fascinated with visible manifestations rather than real power from the Spirit to do God's work. What the New Testament believers wanted most was to receive special ability from God, and any manifestations were unexpected side issues.

The disciples didn't get it at first; you can tell by the prophecy question they asked: "Lord, are you at this time going to restore the kingdom to Israel?" (v. 6). Their curiosity sounds like modern times, doesn't it, with all sorts of books and conferences on the end times but little attention given to our more pressing problems. Jesus flatly told them, "It is not for you to know the times or dates the Father has set by his own authority" (v. 7). He told them to get used to vagueness on these matters. The church's great task is not to clarify what the "mark of the Beast" is, or who the "bear of the North" is, or whether the Jerusalem temple will ever be rebuilt.

Instead, Jesus gave the disciples a divine promise that has never been rescinded: "You will receive power *when* the Holy Spirit comes on you; and you *will be* my witnesses" (v. 8). In other words, the Great Commission of evangelism is the great work of the church—and it will be done only in the power of the Holy Spirit.

What follows after the Ascension, as you know, is that the disciples returned to Jerusalem and began an extended prayer meeting. That was the setting in which the church was born. They patiently waited before God for the power to come upon them and lift them above themselves.

Peter would no longer be Peter the failure; he would be Peter the mighty preacher. He would be transformed, not by learning something new from Scripture, but by experiencing a new dimension of God's Spirit. It would not be mere emotionalism, fanaticism, or psyching himself up to face the challenges ahead. It would be the reality of God supernaturally empowering his servant to accomplish his assigned task.

FROM PASTA TO PREACHING

In some ways Peter's story parallels that of my friend Michael Durso, the pastor of a church, called Christ Tabernacle, that we helped to birth more than fifteen years ago. If you were to go there today, in the Glendale section of Queens, you would find more than 1,500 believers gathered on Sunday to worship the Lord and to affect their needy area of the city for Christ. Many in the congregation do not own cars; they arrive at the church by public transportation. Yet hundreds of them make the effort to come back on Tuesday night for the Christ Tabernacle prayer meeting, a powerful service of calling upon the Lord. (Readers of my previous book *Fresh Faith* will recall that this prayer meeting was where Calvin Hunt dramatically gave his heart to the Lord and was delivered from a raging crack-cocaine habit and into his present life as a gospel singer.)

When Pastor Durso opens his Bible to preach, you would never guess that he, like Peter, didn't come up the normal ministerial route. Raised in an Italian Catholic family, he was the firstborn of three sons destined to inherit the family's gourmet pasta business. Everyone in the area knew that if you wanted the best, freshest linguine or mozzarella for your Sunday feast, Durso's on Utopia Parkway in Flushing was the place to get it. From his teenage years onward, Michael was behind the counter or out making deliveries along with his brothers.

Money was plentiful, and Michael showed an aptitude for making lots of it. His father was pleased. The young man graduated from a Catholic high school and immediately went to work full-time in the family business. After a few years, he had met a girlfriend named Maria, who had inherited a fair amount of money herself. The two of them enjoyed the fast life of high-class drugs in the early seventies.

"We never went to the street to find our drugs; it was always arranged by people coming to meet us in hotel rooms or the apartment where we lived together," Michael explains. "It was all very chic. We especially enjoyed doing cocktails of various drugs mixed together—heroin, quaaludes, acid, cocaine—so we could then boast about it."

Michael was used to taking vacations to exotic resorts where drugs and immorality were the order of the day. One season it would be Tahiti or Bora-Bora in the South Pacific, the next Saint Martin or Guadaloupe in the Caribbean, the next North Africa. Michael's father said little so long as the business stayed healthy—and Michael managed to keep up both ends of his double life.

Then one day, while at a resort in Mexico, Maria made an odd comment: Recently she had been feeling vaguely empty, in spite of all their money and life of pleasure. Maybe when they returned to New York, they should go to church. She said that God seemed to be saying to her, *Give me your life*.

Michael was mildly irritated. He frowned but said okay just to pacify her. "After all, I didn't want her copping an attitude and turning cold on me while on this vacation."

And that is how the young couple wound up at a Sunday night service in a gospel church in the Bay Ridge section of Brooklyn, accompanied by a couple of Maria's girlfriends who had recently become believers. Michael remembers being in a defiant mood. In fact, he brought drugs with him so they would be handy the minute the church service was over and he could whisk Maria away to a Manhattan club for the rest of the night.

"I dressed as outrageously as I could, in a black form-fitting leather outfit, yellow boots, four earrings in one ear. I mainly wanted to shock these religious people. We marched down to one of the front pews, and as the singing began, I hammed it up, clapping with gusto. When it was time to greet those around you, I glad-handed everybody in sight. I was totally obnoxious.

"They had a guest speaker that night, an evangelist from Texas in a western suit with a big cowboy hat. I snickered at his Southern accent. I remember nothing of what he said. I just wanted to get out."

And then … the meeting was being brought to a close with an invitation to receive Christ. All at once, Michael turned sober. "Suddenly, I felt overwhelmed. I knew my life was headed for hell. All my confidence in my religious upbringing and my smart image vanished. I felt ashamed of my appearance. Both Maria and I headed for the front.

"People came around and began praying for us. Both of us started weeping. Soon the pastor approached us and did something very unusual: He anointed our foreheads with oil and then said, 'Lord, I pray that this couple will be used by you in the days and years ahead.' We were perplexed by that."

> "Suddenly, I felt overwhelmed. I knew my life was headed for hell. All my confidence in my religious upbringing and my smart image vanished."
> —Michael Durso

The young couple never made it to a club that evening. Instead, they returned to their sixth-floor apartment and, convicted by the Holy Spirit, began an immediate housecleaning. The building's incinerator chute happened to be just outside their door, and soon they were carrying loads of items to dump. "Nobody told us to do this—but we just knew. First it was a stack of questionable magazines. Next it was our music collection. Then all the drug paraphernalia—the syringes, the gold spoons for snorting cocaine, etc.—went down the chute. There was also jewelry that had been stolen.

"Finally we turned to our closets. Many items were plainly sensual and needed to be tossed. I had a custom-made antelope-leather shirt that was very expensive, with etchings of women on each shoulder, that I knew I had to discard. By midnight we had put thousands and thousands of dollars into the incinerator. I had a fleeting thought of *You know, maybe we could at least sell some of this stuff for money—or give it to our friends.* But then I realized that no, it had to be destroyed."

Before the end of the week, Michael had moved out of the apartment to return to his parents' home until a legitimate wedding could be arranged. The young couple didn't seem to think of any options other than going to a justice of the peace at City Hall in Manhattan on a Monday morning—Monday being the one day of the week when the Durso business was closed.

In time Michael and Maria came to the Brooklyn Tabernacle and began to seek grounding in the Christian faith. We noticed in both of them a heart to follow God, to study his Word, and to give evidence of his grace and love. Michael became an usher in the church, while Maria helped with the teenagers. Next they organized a street ministry, taking groups from the choir and other workers to do outdoor concerts in the summer. In the winter the same groups would be taken to prisons for ministry. Whenever we needed help for a task, Michael was willing to take time off from work and pitch in.

Their growth in God was evident over the years as they carefully studied their Bibles, always joined in our worship and prayer services, and showed giftings from God in ministering to others. No one was too low, too dirty, or too far gone. They knew from their own lives that with God, nothing was impossible.

Years went by, and in 1984 the board of a struggling church in the Greenpoint part of Brooklyn approached me and offered to turn over their building and their $25,000 in the bank if I would promise to oversee the work as long as I was alive. It was a wonderful gift from God, and our pastoral staff began to pray about how best to start a new church in this area. We all sensed the Spirit of God directing our attention to Michael and his wife to spearhead the new venture.

When I finally went over to Michael and Maria's house on a Friday night to say I felt that they should pastor this work, they could hardly believe what I was suggesting. This could mean eventually leaving the lucrative family business. And Michael didn't have the seminary training that ministers are expected to have.

But I believed in my heart that they had something vital: the anointing of the Holy Spirit, and humble hearts to seek God's will.

Time has proven that this appointment was definitely what God wanted. We sent thirty or so of our members with Michael to help begin, and the little church grew and grew until it had to relocate. Today it meets in a converted theater and is one of the strongest lighthouses in our city, touching people for Christ in a powerful way.

THE POWER WE NEED MOST

The God who empowered Simon Peter and Michael Durso is the same God who is waiting to empower us. The needs today to confront the works of darkness are greater than they have ever been. The influence of filth and violence in people's lives will not be destroyed by polite talk. There is a divine antidote to the demonic powers that stir up young people to shoot up schools and worship dark impulses. Our only hope is in the power of the Holy Spirit.

The great Baptist preacher Charles Spurgeon admitted, "Without the Spirit of God we can do nothing. We are as ships without wind or chariots without steeds. Like branches without sap, we are withered. Like coals without fire, we are useless."[7]

Slick organization, barbecues, and theater productions in the church may have their place, but how in the world will they combat the rampant evil around us today? How will they break the stranglehold of materialism in people's lives? The idea that the church is just a teaching center, or a place to escape from the world, is not the right picture. We have a mission from Jesus himself, and only the outpouring of the Spirit's power will enable us to make a difference.

The promise of this divine ability in Acts 1:8 was, in fact, the last thing Jesus said before his ascension. Whenever his disciples thought back to that memorable moment, this word kept ringing in their ears: *You will receive power. . . . You will be my witnesses. . . . You will receive power. . . . You will be my witnesses. . . .* Their Lord had promised to supernaturally equip them to establish his kingdom in Judea, Jerusalem, and Samaria, and to the ends of the earth.

THREE

Something from Heaven

IMAGINE THAT BY SOME time-warp technology you could zoom back two thousand years to the upper room in Jerusalem a week after the ascension of our Lord. As you stand there in a corner, I want you to take a close look at the men and women sitting in this place. Scan the crowd and look into their faces. What do you see? Think about who they are and where they come from.

The first obvious question would be about the apostles and why the Lord Jesus chose these particular men as leaders. Why didn't he select rabbis and scholars of the Law? He could have chosen gifted orators who could sway thousands with their powers of speech. Instead, you see fishermen. You see a former tax collector. You see a former member of the Zealots, a radical political group. You see ordinary men. No executive search process would ever have selected them for such crucial leadership. These are the last people you would pick to launch a religious movement.

Of course, Jesus did this on purpose. He knew it would be almost impossible for them to depend on their human ability; instead, they would have to reach out to his promise of "power from on high." He recognized that all too often the more educated people become, and the brighter they are, and the better their connections to human influence, money, and power ... the more they tend to look away from the power of God. They trust in God's grace less and less.

Even worse than what I have already described is that this upper-room group included men of recent spiritual failure. Just a few weeks ago, at a moment of crisis, they deserted their leader. Their three-year discipleship experience under the teaching of Jesus suddenly went out the window. All the lessons they had learned (and who could have taught truth more perfectly and brilliantly than the Son of God?) seemed to count for nothing. They had watched his example in every kind of circumstance; they had seen him stand up to pressure in the midst of vigorous debate with the Pharisees; they had held their breath as he courageously cast out the powers of darkness. Yet, when their own hour of crisis came, they bailed out. When push came to shove, they ran for the shadows. All the good teaching and good example evaporated into the nighttime chill of Gethsemane.

And not only did they show a surprising cowardice, but one of them, Peter, lurched into a full-blown denial of Jesus. In fact, three times he said he didn't even know Christ—the last time punctuated with profanity.

A couple of days later, when Thomas was told that Christ had come back from the dead, he was so steeped in doubt and self-pity that he replied, in essence, "No way! That's impossible."

Would you want to build any kind of a future on this group? I wouldn't.

A FORLORN LOT

Yet there these men sit in the upper room, simply waiting, praying, perhaps singing at times. A deep sense of aloneness claws at their spirits. Memories of Jesus flit across the inner screen of their minds ... the time Jesus walked on the water, the time he stilled the storm, the times he fed huge crowds. Now all that is in the distant past, and Jesus is far away somewhere ... they don't really know where.

They are tormented by reminders of how they failed their Master in his neediest hour. Maybe they should just go outside and disperse. But that could be dangerous, couldn't it? They are, after all, in the middle of Jerusalem, the city that just cried out for Jesus to be crucified and certainly has no love for his former followers. What will become of them after all?

Yes, he had said as he left them that they would receive some kind of *power* when the Holy Spirit came upon them (whatever that might mean) and would be his witnesses to the ends of the earth. But how could that happen? Who was this other Counselor who would be with them forever and make them into mighty men of God? Surely some unimaginable, powerful someone or something would have to change them into spiritual champions.

And then the Scripture tells us:

> When the day of Pentecost came, they were all together in one place. Suddenly a sound like the blowing of a violent wind came from heaven and filled the whole house where they were sitting. They saw what seemed to be tongues of fire that separated and came to rest on each of them. All of them were filled with the Holy Spirit and began to speak in other tongues as the Spirit enabled them (Acts 2:1–4).

I am not so much concerned to focus on the individual phenomena here—the wind, the fire, the speaking in tongues—as I am to hold up the main truth that *something supernatural came from heaven and invaded men and women on earth, changing them forever.*

I think we have lost the wonder of that because we are so familiar with the passage. Since the Holy Spirit *is* God, what is the depth of meaning in those words "all of them *were filled with the Holy Spirit*"? They were filled with God himself!

Forget for a moment what you have been taught by others about this phrase. Open yourself to what God did here. Frail men and women were not just given help around the edges, but were *filled* with God the Holy Spirit.

POWER FOR THE PRESENT

Who can deny that this is the great need in our churches today? This is what all pastors desperately require, starting with me. We need something with the mark of heaven upon it. Too much of our religious life is made up of programs and human ideas, talents and strategies. While these have value, they pitifully fail to meet the need of the hour. What is missing today is something from heaven itself, something from God the Holy Spirit that fills and floods our lives.

> Too much of our religious life is made up of programs and human ideas, talents and strategies.... What is missing today is something from heaven itself.

This has always been God's design for his church. Take, for example, the Bible's statement "If anyone speaks, he should do it as one speaking the very words of God" (1 Peter 4:11). How long has it been since you heard that kind of authoritative, heart-searching preaching? Instead, too many church meetings have become increasingly predictable and dull. Many enemies of Christianity over the centuries have become confirmed in their agnostic opinions by going to churches that purported to be "Christian" but were dreadfully barren and spiritually dead. How could God be real and powerful if this kind of church was his major advertisement? Never mind just quoting verses from the Bible; they were looking for some sign of Christianity working itself out through real flesh and blood.

Many people today, even church members, agree with the critics, although they're too polite to say so. Everything in the service may be doctrinally sound—but there's nothing *from heaven* that grips them. Too often we are found discussing only words and phrases, doctrinal positions and denominational traditions—but where is the power of the Holy Spirit in all of this?

By contrast, we see the New Testament church and its ministers regularly having encounters with the living God. This sense of the divine brought hardened sinners to their knees. The powerful word stabbed their consciences. The Holy Spirit produced a climate that was anything but dull and ordinary.

And in fact, this kind of anointed preaching evoked controversy. The upstanding citizens of at least one city, Thessalonica, moaned, "These men who have caused trouble all over the world have now come here" (Acts 17:6). It is sadly the same in our churches today. The very mention of God's promise of "something from heaven" makes people nervous if it seems that the boat might get rocked or if there might be a departure from the order of service printed in the church bulletin.

But have you ever been in a meeting where, let's say, a song touched your heart in a probing yet tender way? It wasn't just a combination of lyrics and notes; it was a message made alive to you by the Holy Spirit. Have you ever sat listening to a sermon that stirred your heart to its depths and spoke powerfully to your own spiritual need? You sat there saying to yourself, *There's no way this speaker could know what I'm like or how I'm struggling right now. And yet this message is like he's been reading my mail. God must have told him what to say today.*

WIND, FIRE, VOICE

What God did on the Day of Pentecost was dramatic and powerful. One of the biblical symbols of the Holy Spirit is wind, and the wind in the upper room that day wasn't just a little breeze; it was "violent," according to Acts 2:2. In many of us, we need just such a strong wind to blow out the rubbish that has accumulated. Many of our churches need a typhoonlike visitation of the Spirit of God. We need a major renovation of our spiritual lives, not just a rearrangement of the furniture. Think how whole cities and towns would be affected if Christian churches began praying for the wind of God to blow upon them.

Fire is another Holy Spirit symbol, and tongues of fire formed that day over each of the 120 heads in the room—men and women alike. It wasn't the apostles alone. God the Holy Spirit visited each believer, since all of them needed his power equally to accomplish God's will for their individual lives.

After that, the people in the upper room spoke in languages they did not know except as "the Spirit enabled them" (v. 4). The ecstatic tongues that flowed from these ordinary people were identified by visitors from all around the Mediterranean who had come to Jerusalem that week. The immediate result of their baptism with the Holy Spirit was that they began to do something they could not normally do.

Without getting into the debates that have arisen about speaking in tongues, let us focus on the main point of this passage: God by his Spirit enabled ordinary men and women to do and say things beyond their natural abilities. They became supernaturally empowered. There was no human explanation for what was taking place.

This is the story, in one way or another, of every man, woman, or church that has ever been used in great ways for God's glory. They were set on fire by God, and that experience affected the world around them.

Praise God for his ability to lift us above ourselves! Otherwise, where would all of us be? Especially people such as my wife, Carol, and me, who never got to go to a Bible college or seminary ... others who say, "I don't have this talent or that ability." We can take courage from the fact that these fishermen and others—"losers" by the world's standards—were invaded by God and raised to amazing places. The same tongues that had engaged in petty argument about who was the greatest, the same tongues that had denied the Lord and the fact of his resurrection were now overtaken by heaven itself and put to use "declaring the wonders of God" (v. 11).

The Holy Spirit is still greater today than all our shortcomings and failures. He has come to free us from the restraints and complexes of insufficient talent, intelligence, or upbringing. He intends to do through us what only he can do. The issue is not our ability but rather our availability to the person of the Holy Spirit.

In fact, this is God's ordained way of equipping us, because it leaves little doubt about who should get all the glory. If our human intellect and abilities and talents produced the results, we could strut around saying, "My, we're pretty special, don't you think?" (By the way, that is the very attitude of too many churches that are run on the basis of programs and human talent rather than the manifest power of the Holy Spirit.)

But men and women who are truly used by God are necessarily humbled, because they know the true source of their strength. Think of how Peter and the others rejoiced that night as they fell asleep in their beds. God's grace and the

power of the Spirit had proven greater than their human failure and limitations.

Jesus told the disciples one time, "When they arrest you,
do not worry about what to say or how to say it. At that time
you will be given what to say, for it will not be you speaking,
but the Spirit of your Father speaking through you" (Matthew
10:19–20). We see this happening time and again in the book
of Acts, not only for Peter and Paul but for others such as
Stephen: They are hauled into court, and from their lips comes
suddenly a message with the mark of the Holy Spirit upon it.

I am not against sermon notes and outlines for ministers.
But isn't it tragic that many pastors often spend hours polish-
ing every nuance of their sermons while hardly investing
much time at all in prayer and waiting upon God to be freshly
filled with the One who can supernaturally assist them? What
we need today is not cleverness or oratory—we need messages from God's Word set on fire by the Holy Spirit!

D. L. Moody, as you may know, never had the formal
credentials to be ordained. That is why he was always called
simply "Mr. Moody." He was short, stocky, and not particu-
larly attractive in appearance. He mispronounced words regularly. If you read his personal letters, you will see all kinds
of punctuation and spelling errors.

Yet he addressed more people and brought more of them
to Christ than anyone else in the nineteenth century. How
did that happen?

Well, Moody said that the turning point was something
that happened just across the East River from the borough of
Brooklyn, where our church is located—while he was walking on Wall Street no less! In late 1871, just a few weeks after
the great Chicago fire, the thirty-four-year-old Moody had
come east to try to raise money to rebuild the buildings he
had lost. But, he writes,

My heart was not in the work of begging. I could not appeal. I was crying all the time that God would fill me with His Spirit. Well, one day, in the city of New York—oh, what a day!—I cannot describe it. I seldom refer to it; it is almost too sacred an experience to name.... I can only say that God revealed Himself to me, and I had such an experience of His love that I had to ask Him to stay His hand. I went to preaching again. The sermons were not different; I did not present any new truths, and yet hundreds were converted. I would not now be placed back where I was before that blessed experience if you should give me all the world.[1]

Oh, that all of us might receive, like Mr. Moody, something fresh from the Holy Spirit that revolutionizes our spiritual lives!

A Curious Crowd

The coming of the Spirit upon the disciples and his divine enablement brought a large crowd together, the first such audience that showed any interest in the followers of the recently crucified Jesus. Crowds will always gather when the Holy Spirit is working in the midst of God's people. Peter recognized the evangelistic opportunity and stood up to preach. How would he do?

This was a man who had little, if any, formal education and was by trade a fisherman. This was the one who less than two months before had vociferously renounced the Lord. This was the man who, even after seeing the resurrected Lord, opted to forget the ministry and go back to fishing (John 21). This was the man who in sensitive situations was infamous for putting his foot in his mouth. What respectable church today would let this man into its pulpit! Can you hear the introduction, "Congregation, let's give a warm welcome today to Brother Peter, who just a few months ago denied he even knew Jesus . . ."? I doubt it.

In fact, Peter spoke marvelously with clarity and power. He quoted both the prophet Joel and the book of Psalms at length, apparently from memory. When he finished, the crowd was "cut to the heart" and began to call out, "What shall we do?" (v. 37). By the end of the meeting, some three thousand people had been saved. Not a bad first outing for the rookie preacher.

What made the difference? The only variable in the equation was that now Peter had been taken over by the Holy Spirit. It is staggering to remember that Peter walked with Jesus for three years and received teaching, discipleship, and a moral example unparalleled in all of history. And yet all of that never made Peter the man God intended him to be. It is not until we see Peter "filled with the Holy Spirit" that things really turned around. No wonder Jesus excitedly assured them that greater days were coming for all of them when the Holy Spirit, their invisible Helper, came upon them in power.

> **It is not enough to teach and preach about the Spirit. We must experience him personally in new depths, or we will accomplish little.**

As Samuel Chadwick succinctly put it, "The Christian religion is hopeless without the Holy Ghost."[2]

To that I would add, ministry is especially hopeless without the Holy Spirit. Let every pastor take note: Our attempt at ministry will be an absolute exercise in futility if we are not expecting and experiencing divine help through the power of the Holy Spirit.

It is not enough to teach and preach about the Spirit. We must experience him personally in new depths, or we will accomplish little. Without the Holy Spirit there is no quickening of the Scripture. Worship is hollow. Preaching is mechanical, never piercing the heart. Conviction of sin is almost nonexistent. Faith is more mental than heartfelt. Prayer meetings fade away. Church meetings become routine. And Christian people stay lukewarm at best.

Please, God, send the Holy Spirit upon us and revive your people.

I am not issuing any kind of call for fanaticism. We don't need musicians working up the audience into some kind of frenzy. We don't need manipulated manifestations or counterfeit gifts. But we do need the real Holy Spirit upon us in power, in all our churches, of all denominations and traditions.

Listen to Chadwick's bold indictment from a century ago:

> The church still has a theology of the Holy Spirit, but it has no living consciousness of his presence and power. Theology without experience is like faith without works: it is dead. The signs of death abound. Prayer meetings have died out because men did not believe in the Holy Ghost. The liberty of prophesying has gone because men believe in investigation and not in inspiration. There is a dearth of conversions because faith about the new birth as a creative act of the Holy Ghost has lost its grip on intellect and heart. The experience of the second gift of grace is no longer preached and testified because Christian experience, though it may have to begin in the Spirit, must be perfected in the wisdom of the flesh and the culture of the schools. Confusion and impotence are the inevitable results when the wisdom and resources of the world

are substituted for the presence and power of the Spirit.[3]

What Christian here in the new millennium cannot agree that we desperately need a fresh filling of the Holy Spirit? Isn't that the heart-cry of Scripture, even long before the book of Acts? The prophet Isaiah pleaded with God,

> Oh, that you would rend the heavens and come down,
>   that the mountains would tremble before you!
> As when fire sets twigs ablaze
>   and causes water to boil,
> come down to make your name known to your enemies
>   and cause the nations to quake before you!
> For when you did awesome things that we did not
>   expect,
>   you came down, and the mountains trembled before
>   you.
> Since ancient times no one has heard,
>   no ear has perceived,
> no eye has seen any God besides you,
>   who acts on behalf of those who wait for him (Isaiah
>   64:1–4).

How long has it been in many of our churches since God "did awesome things that we did not expect"? Maybe it is because we have not done what the last line suggests, in waiting before God as they did in the upper room. The Christian life, like the life of Jesus on earth, is a combination of waiting and activity, of prayer and service. Jesus spent time alone with the Father in solitary places and then went forth in power to face incredibly busy days of ministry to needy people. Likewise, we must balance all our activities *for* him with time spent *with* him, waiting in expectant prayer and worship. We must avoid the idea that well-intentioned Christian service and doing things for God will ever amount to much without fresh infillings of the Spirit's power.

Admittedly, we must also beware of the opposite: a pseudospiritual life of spending time alone with God without ever getting out among the people and laboring with all our strength to bring them the gospel. Consider the proper biblical balance of human effort and dependence upon the Spirit's power: "To this end *I labor*, struggling with all *his energy*, which so powerfully works *in me*" (Colossians 1:29). Would to God that more of us ministers could honestly say this verse about our own lives.

CRY OF THE HEART

What stops us today from drawing a line in the sand and setting our hearts toward God in fervent prayer that he will come and revive his work in us as well as in our churches? Soon our lives will be over, and it is better to live a few years full of the Spirit, seeing God work in and through us, than to go on for decades with little or no experience of the great things God has promised to his people through the person and work of the Spirit.

In a world as tormented and confused as ours, we desperately need God's wind and fire to energize us. With sin on the rampage and demonic powers controlling more and more of our culture, we need an enduement of divine power similar to what God gave the early church. Why don't we stop rationalizing and justifying the spiritual impotence all around us? Why not rather humble ourselves and seek God with all our heart for "something from heaven"?

....

Dear Father, please stir our hearts to reach out for all that you have promised us. Forgive our carnality, our indifference to the spiritual realities around us, and our dependence on human resources rather than your power. Teach us to pray and wait upon you in humility and faith; send the wind and fire of your Spirit upon us. Transform us into men and women who bear powerful witness in word and deed to the reality of Jesus Christ our Savior. We ask all of this in his precious name. Amen.

FOUR

Spirit-Fueled Preaching

ONE OF THE GREAT problems I face as a pastor in the inner city is a misunderstanding about a very common word. The word is *father*. This term, of course, has major theological implications for believers in Christ, who taught us to pray, "Our Father in heaven. . . ." The New Testament describes God's relationship to us as "Father" in hundreds of places.

Many people who come to Christ in our church, however, need a major renewing of their minds in order to properly understand what "Father" means in Scripture. Their upbringing has unfortunately locked them into a distorted concept. In many cases their own biological father was a drug addict, an alcoholic, someone who abused their mother in front of them—or perhaps someone they never knew at all. You can quickly see how these new believers have real problems with the word *father*.

God, of course, is not like their earthly father at all, so the Holy Spirit has to reveal to them that God is loving and merciful in a way beyond anything they have ever known.

But I am convinced that other important words in our faith suffer from similar distortion due to our personal experience in church over the years. Using our denominational or church tradition, we have tended to absorb our definitions and mental pictures of words such as *worship, prayer, evangelism,* or *preaching* from our religious environment rather than from the Word of God. God might have something far different and greater in mind, but we are limited by our upbringing. Instead of prayerfully searching the Scriptures and asking for the Spirit's help, we just assume that our church culture has given us the proper definition of these words. However, I am not sure we are as accurate and biblically sound as we might think.

Don't we all need a fresh breaking and humbling before God so we can receive revelation of how he intended things to be? We must remember that it is *his* kingdom to be established and *his* work to be done on the earth. So the question is, What did he have in mind when he gave us his purpose and plan through the inspired Scriptures? For example, the whole idea of the church was his in the beginning, not ours. He gave us the book of Acts and the epistles to show how the church began in power and fruitfulness and can continue in the same way. The more we come with open minds and hearts to learn, the more he will teach us about his purpose for our individual and local-church lives.

WHAT'S GOING ON?

On the Day of Pentecost, the crowd came together in bewilderment. They were drawn by what the Holy Spirit was doing in the church. The principle here is that audiences are best gathered by the unexplainable work of the Holy Spirit. As Luke puts it in Acts 2:12, they were "amazed and perplexed."

When the Spirit of God is showing himself strong on behalf of his people, it gathers other people who ask, "How is this happening?" The Christian church and its meetings are greater than the sum of their parts. They are greater than the various talents of the participants. My friend, the noted author Warren Wiersbe, says, "If you can fully explain a church, then something's wrong." In other words, if a church is only methodology and organizational technique and clever advertising, it is departing from what God planned it to be. There should always be the element of supernatural assistance that is unexplainable to the natural mind.

The church in the book of Acts "didn't add up." Peter and the others shouldn't have been able to achieve what they achieved. As the priests and Sadducees noted, these "were unschooled, ordinary men" (Acts 4:13). But they were effective nonetheless because God the Holy Spirit was working through them.

> If a church is only methodology and organizational technique and clever advertising, it is departing from what God planned it to be. There should always be the element of supernatural assistance.

Paul explains in 1 Corinthians 3:16, "Don't you know that you yourselves are God's temple and that God's Spirit lives in you?" The "you" at the end of this question is a plural pronoun describing the people of God. The word for "temple" here is the word used for the Holy of Holies in the tabernacle, where the high priest entered only once a year, on the Day of Atonement. It was an awesome place where God's glory showed itself in some visible way. Paul dares to say that we in the church are God's temple.

The great concern of heaven right now is not whether a new temple is going to be rebuilt on the Temple Mount in Jerusalem. God is more interested in whether his church is living out what it was meant to be: the Holy of Holies for his Spirit. He wants the church to be a place of awe and wonder—two qualities that we have largely lost in our meetings.

Peter's sermon brought a sense of deep conviction of sin. The audience was diverse in every way possible, yet one anointed sermon brought thousands to salvation. The Holy

Spirit didn't need a special service for Generation X or a toning down of the message for older traditionalists. Instead, Peter boldly declared that "you, with the help of wicked men, put him [the Messiah] to death by nailing him to the cross" (Acts 2:23). He obviously was ignorant of the crowd-pleasing insights that are now blindly followed in so many churches. No, God brings conviction of sin when the Word of God is preached in the power and love of the Spirit.

Similarly, Paul urged that spiritual gifts be used in such a way that if an unbeliever comes in, "he will be convinced by all that he is a sinner and will be judged by all, and the secrets of his heart will be laid bare. So he will fall down and worship God, exclaiming, 'God is really among you!'" (1 Corinthians 14:24–25). That kind of reaction is not only missing today— we're not even aiming at it. We have lost faith in God's ability to do what he promised through the Spirit.

It saddens my heart when I contrast these New Testament models of Holy Spirit power with today's popular "user-friendly" approaches. Unbelievers can regularly attend meetings and leave with no conviction whatsoever, because neither the Spirit nor the Word has preeminence. Many feel the message must be diluted because they don't want to scare off the visitor; they don't believe the Bible record that plain-spoken truth anointed by the Holy Spirit through a loving vessel will bring men and women to Christ. Instead of concentrating on divine power, they're busy "relating." They strive to meet people "where they are" and tell them what they want to hear. If it's entertainment they want, the church will provide it. Pastors certainly won't step on any toes or make anyone uncomfortable.

Please show me one place where this approach was used in the book of Acts, which was the golden age of the church. Such a mentality is tragic; even worse is that young ministers attend conferences where they learn to implement a philosophy of ministry unknown to the New Testament.

A friend of mine in the Christian music field told me he had recently received a call from a distraught minister of music in the Midwest who had just been roundly scolded by her newly arrived senior pastor. What offense had this woman committed? Nothing more than to have her choir sing the Brooklyn Tabernacle Singers' "Communion Medley," which starts off with "Oh, the Blood of Jesus" and then continues on to "Wash Me in the Fountain" and then the old hymn "Nothing But the Blood of Jesus."

Said the senior pastor to the woman, his voice rising: "You will *never, ever* sing about the blood of Jesus in this church again! If you do, you will lose your job. We've outgrown the stage of using crude religious symbols from another era."

What a horrible grieving of the Spirit of God!

MORE POWER, LESS SHOW

The connection between preaching and the work of the Holy Spirit is explained by Paul when he describes his ministry in Corinth: "My message and my preaching were not with wise and persuasive words, but with a demonstration of the Spirit's power, so that your faith might not rest on men's wisdom, but on God's power" (1 Corinthians 2:4–5). Think of these words today when so many speakers and churches *want* to produce "wise and persuasive words," cleverness and human charisma, a beautiful church plant and great programs for the family—everything but the "demonstration of the Spirit's power" that the apostle Paul exalted to the glory of God.

I am personally stirred as I meditate on this passage, because very possibly what we call "preaching" is hardly at all what God intended it to be. So much of it is showy; so much is cowardly, not confronting people with God's holiness and the sinfulness of sin so that grace can be appreciated; so much is simply a kind of religious performance with little sense of sincerity, heartfelt passion from God, or evidence of the Spirit. Too many are obsessed with making everyone feel comfortable, whereas apostolic preaching was often the exact opposite.

E. M. Bounds, a Methodist minister of a hundred years ago, had it exactly right when he wrote,

> The power of Christ's dispensation is a fiery pulpit—not a learned pulpit, not a popular pulpit, not an eloquent pulpit, but a pulpit on fire with the Holy Ghost. . . .
>
> This power is not the mere iteration or reiteration of truth well learned or well told, but it is the enabling force to declare revealed truth with superhuman authority. The preacher must have the power given by direct connection with God. . . .
>
> God does not mix this power with other solutions to give it efficiency. It is not some or much of the Holy Ghost mixed with some or much of other ingredients. This power is from the Holy Ghost singular and alone. It is the one thing to be sought and secured, the one thing whose importance discredits all other things, the one thing that stands alone unrivaled and supreme.[1]

I don't know about you, but I would rather run the risk of some people even mocking me (as in Acts 2) than to shortchange the gospel of Christ and the Holy Spirit. I would rather be labeled a fanatic along with the apostles than to build a reputation on slickness. At least they were able to produce converts who *"devoted themselves* to the apostles' teaching and to the fellowship, to the breaking of bread and to prayer" (v. 42), which is more than a lot of modern congregations can claim. We have institutionalized backsliddenness to the point that the book of Acts shocks us. Some even make up theological excuses by saying, "All that 'power stuff' was just for back then before they had all sixty-six books of the Bible completed." What a pathetic cop-out. What a rejection of the very Bible they boast in.

> I would rather be labeled a fanatic along with the apostles than to build a reputation on slickness.

All of this is due to the absence of the Holy Spirit in the meetings. We are not welcoming him and counting on his ministry among us. Instead, the supposed sensitivities of the audience hold sway. It is almost as if we were selling bread or cigarettes or computers—the customer is king. If we don't keep the people engaged and amused, they will go down the block to the next church, where there's a better display. What a dreary concept of Christian ministry! At the root of all this foolishness is no acquaintance or experience with the living Spirit of God.

No wonder we are sometimes even mocked by the secular world. A "Doonesbury" cartoon shows the trendy Rev Scott in his office explaining to a young man, "It's an interesting congregation, Mike. Members are far more consumer-conscious than they used to be. The church has to deliver for its members! Counseling, social events, recovery programs, tutoring, fitness center—we have to have it all!"

Mike: "Where's God fit into all this?"

Rev Scott: "God? Well, God's still the draw, for sure. He's got the big name."

Mike: "But do you ever evoke it anymore?"

Rev Scott: "Um . . . frankly, Mike, God comes with a lot of baggage. The whole male, Eurocentric guilt thing. . . ."

How tragic! A group of people calling themselves Christians but uneasy about putting Christ in the forefront because he might say something about sin or repentance or the need to be changed.

By contrast, look at Peter's sermon—the first ever preached in church history under the anointing of the Holy Spirit. This is obviously a new Peter—no longer a flop or failure. He boldly tells the crowd that what they are seeing and hearing is a long-awaited fulfillment of Joel's prophecy. Here are men and women, he explains, who have become the human temples of God's very presence. They have been filled up with the Holy Spirit the way Solomon's temple was once filled up with smoke.

This is unique among the world's religions. Buddhism, Islam, and the rest pay honor and respect to a god, or gods. But the gods remain "out there" at a safe distance; they don't come and fill up redeemed worshipers in an intimate, dynamic way. This is the unique note of Christianity.

NO RHYMES, NO PLASTIC SMILE

What is a Spirit-filled preacher? Many of us have heard oratory and cleverness in the pulpit. We've seen showmanship and listened to smoothly worded phrases. In contrast to all this, here is Peter, a fisherman with no formal training in homiletics, giving a simple but powerful message.

It is totally unprepared. Peter has no notes, obviously. (Throughout the book of Acts, seldom does the preacher know in advance that he's going to have to speak; the occasion just pops up, and he opens his mouth in expectation that God will fill it.) Still, Peter begins in the common language of the people to declare the gospel.

He has no rhyming outline, no alliterations, no soothing poems. He is bold as he moves ahead. He is not afraid to confront his listeners. Yet he is also loving and compassionate. He drives straight toward the need for each person to decide what to do about Jesus Christ.

His message is not Law-centered but Christ-centered. He doesn't push for people to join the church. He doesn't call for the audience to promise to do better. Instead, he points them to the Savior, urging them to repent, put their faith in Christ, be baptized—"and you will receive the gift of the Holy Spirit" (v. 38), the same thing the 120 had already received in the upper room.

No waiting period to show themselves worthy or holy enough—just believe and receive . . . and then keep on believing and receiving from God for the rest of their lives.

In the end, we see his heart: "With many other words he warned them; and he pleaded with them" (v. 40). He wasn't just performing. His heart had been filled with love of God through the Holy Spirit, so he saw these people and felt their needs in a new, divine way. No plastic ministerial smile or glad-handing for Peter. The first ministers were not "professionals" or shallow "preaching machines," but rather servants of the people and God.

On the other extreme, we have all seen preachers who fake emotion and put a tear in their voice. This is just an alternate form of stagecraft. Preachers should humbly present Jesus and then sink out of sight so people can get to Christ at the throne of grace. Instead, we often see *preachers* as the centerpiece of the action, directing attention to themselves, boastful, proud, and often using sacrilegious gimmicks to fleece the sheep of their money. This is all millions of miles from what God intended the preaching of the gospel to be.

By the way, isn't it amazing that no strong voices are raised in charismatic circles and the religious media against charlatans who use the name of Christ to swindle people out of their money? Have you ever read the appeal letters or watched the TV fund-raising that border on (or cross over) the line of out-right lying and blasphemy? I received a classic letter from a well-known evangelist who said God had "shown" him that "a new anointing" was now available for his people, and it could be mine for sending in $33.33 to receive the evangelist's prayers and a particular religious trinket. But beyond that, if I could come up with $99.99, I could then receive a "triple anointing"! (There must have been a special monthly sale or something.)

> **Preachers should humbly present Jesus and then sink out of sight so people can get to Christ at the throne of grace.**

This was not an obscure person but a teacher-preacher who appears regularly on Christian television. I was shocked at the audacity, the deception, and the greed of it all. People such as this would have been stoned in Old Testament times. But today the waters are so polluted that it hardly even raises eyebrows.

I read the appeal letter to my congregation and warned them that any offer of God's blessing, healing, or anointing connected to a dollar donation is a scam and utterly shameful. Jesus taught, "Freely you have received, freely give" (Matthew 10:8). I learned from a friend that it is a common practice among ministers of this ilk not even to write the words that appear over their signatures. They are instead composed by professional ghostwriters who concoct a new gimmick each month to bilk mostly poor and uneducated people out of their hard-earned money. These crooks should be rebuked, shamed, and shunned by all thinking Christians according to scriptural instruction. They are frauds and will find out in the end that the crowd kept outside the gates of the heavenly city for all eternity includes not only murderers and idolaters but also "everyone who loves and practices falsehood" (Revelation 22:15).

Peter was putting on no such shameful show. He was utterly sincere in his pleading. The moment was not so much psychological as it was spiritual.

He was also daring in his conclusion. He didn't shrink from calling people to repentance and new life in the Spirit. "The promise is for you and your children and for all who are far off—for all whom the Lord our God will call," he affirmed (Acts 2:39). No possibly's, maybe's, or hope-so's. He was bold and confident in preaching God's truth.

THE EFFECT

What was the effect on the crowd? They were "cut to the heart" (v. 37). Another translation says "stabbed." They were humbled and broken. Nobody came prancing up to Peter saying, "Well, I'll come back if next time you'll give me this or that." Spirit-filled, anointed preaching brings us down before God so that he can, as promised, "lift you up" (James 4:10). Self-righteousness is gone. Pretense is demolished. It's either that or the opposite reaction of outright rejection.

Catherine Booth, "Mother of the Salvation Army," said once while preaching at City Temple, London, "The greatest want in this day is truth that cuts—convincing truth—truth that convicts and convinces the sinner and pulls off the bandages from his eyes."

That was exactly what happened in the book of Acts—people either got in or got out. Either they were broken down before the Lord or else they turned away and maligned the message. Spirit-empowered preaching cuts to the heart of the matter and brings resolution to spiritual issues. Peter was no bull in a china shop, but he did preach the truth as it is in Jesus.

Yes, all true preaching must have solid, biblical content—but that is not enough. The message must come through a messenger filled with the Holy Spirit. Otherwise people will sit in church pews year after year without ever coming in contact with the true "sword of the Spirit, which is the word of God" (Ephesians 6:17). Please notice that the Word of God is not the "sword of the preacher" but is effectively used only in the hands of the Holy Spirit, who must apply it to human hearts in power. This is what the great Scottish devotional writer Andrew Bonar meant in 1877 when he appealed to the preachers of his generation: "Let us put ourselves under the Holy Spirit's teaching anew, to be taught the Word, and how to preach the Word, not our thoughts upon it. One spark of lightning is worth a thousand of tame candle flames; so one sentence given by the Holy Ghost is worth volumes of any other."[2]

We have all sat through too many meetings where the message was doctrinally correct, but we still were tempted to doze off. Some of us have also seen ministers acting like maniacs trying to imitate supposed effects of the Holy Spirit, and we were embarrassed. No wonder so many buildings today are half-empty. There is no power, no presence of the Spirit, no awe. Nobody's heart is stabbed—the divine surgery that cuts away cancers and brings healing to the soul.

E. M. Bounds explained,

> An anointed pulpit is the mightiest agency that God has in this world. It is God's representative, the representative of his holiness, of his power, of his justice, and of his mercy. An anointed ministry is a ministry consecrated and qualified to the great work by the power of the Holy Ghost. The divine call confers the right, the distinguished privilege to preach; the anointing qualifies to

preach. The disciples received their call to preach under the personal ministry of Christ. The qualifying power was not received until the Pentecostal anointing.[3]

What was the result of Peter's sermon? No less than 3,000 conversions. People were radically transformed by the power of the gospel preached with the supernatural help of the Holy Spirit. All of this came, of course, after a wonderful prayer meeting in which the disciples had secured the wonderful promise of the Father. This has remained the pattern for two thousand years. Christians meet to seek the Lord, and then somehow, some way, the gospel begins to spread in power, changing lives wherever it goes.

This is why we must go back quickly to God's pattern for revival, blessing, and successful evangelism. We must return to prayer, not only personal and private but also corporate and public. God has promised us all an abundant supply of the Spirit—rivers, floods, and oceans—rather than trying to live off meager drops now and again from his fountain.

WHAT TRULY CHANGES PEOPLE

God has given us a very simple equation if only we have the faith to reach out and experience it:

1. The Holy Spirit's power is our greatest need.
2. This power and blessing is freely promised to all of God's people.
3. This promise can only be fully received through sincere praying in faith and through waiting on God for his blessing to come.

This is what happened in the New Testament, and this is the only thing that will satisfy our souls' thirst. People have turned back to these spiritual "facts of life" countless times throughout the centuries as prayer for spiritual revival has ascended to heaven from hungry believers on earth. Read the history of the Christian church, and you will see that the greatest times of evangelism and extension of God's kingdom have come in times of spiritual revival—"times of refreshing . . . from the presence of the Lord" (Acts 3:19 NKJV).

The Old Testament declaration is still 100 percent true today: It is "'not by might nor by power, but by my Spirit,' says the LORD Almighty" (Zechariah 4:6). A decade of gadgets and gimmicks will never accomplish what God the Holy Spirit can do in one month as he works in the life of a church.

> A decade of gadgets and gimmicks will never accomplish what God the Holy Spirit can do in one month.

A pastor in Louisiana read *Fresh Wind, Fresh Fire* and got so convicted about the absence of the Spirit's power in his church that he decided to start weekly prayer meetings. Sadly, within a few weeks the church split over this! His opponents said, "Don't you know that we are _____ [a certain denomination], and we don't have prayer meetings?!" Never mind what the Bible says or what has always brought spiritual renewal to God's people— these folks weren't about to leave the comfortable confines of their religious traditions.

I am sure that those people are convinced that theirs is a Christian church and that their denomination in fact is somehow superior to all others. But can you imagine a church split over the question of having a prayer meeting? The issue was not selling drugs in the sanctuary or denying Christ in a sermon. It was only the pastor's desire to gather regularly to pray—and some folks left the church! The very Bible they carry rebukes them sternly, and it will be written over them in the end, "You quarrel and fight. You do not have, because you do not ask God" (James 4:2).

When Peter preached the first sermon of the Christian era that day, clever human methods didn't bring these converts into the church; God did it through an unlikely spokesman. Preaching experts would look at this sermon and say, "What? It's nothing. We'd be embarrassed to preach such a thing."

Yet, think of the joy that erupted that day over 3,000 new believers. How many homes rejoiced that night. How many daughters and sons found themselves with new fathers who began to love them and care for them rather than ignore them. How many marriages were healed that day.

All this came through the work of the Holy Spirit.

Jesus once said, "'Whoever believes in me, as the Scripture has said, streams of living water will flow from within him.' By this he meant the Spirit, whom those who believed in him were later to receive" (John 7:38–39). This overflow is what brings blessing to other people and, indeed, the whole world. And no case is too hard for God. The gospel of Christ with the power of the Spirit can transform the hardest cases imaginable.

Take, for example, the case of Willie McLean. Standing six-feet-four, he is our church's head of security and walks with me every Sunday as I move in and out of our four crowded services. What an irony that he should be serving God in this line of work, since his "rap sheet" with the NYPD is, as the saying goes, as long as your arm. If you read it, you would say Willie was absolutely hopeless, truly incorrigible—just lock him up and throw away the key. Yet, today he is a dedicated man in God's service, even as he still carries in his body two bullets the surgeons have never removed—one in his back, the other in his jaw.

I won't take the time and space to tell you his full story; he's lived at least three or four lives already. Suffice it to give you just a few snapshots:

....

Willie started off horribly in junior high by getting his girlfriend pregnant—the twelve-year-old daughter of a New York City cop. "I didn't know she was only twelve," he says with a shy smile. When Elise gave birth to the baby, her parents tried to keep things quiet . . . until the next year, when the young couple did it again!

This time the irate father had Willie arrested for statutory rape. In front of the Family Court judge, however, the thirteen-year-old Elise—just released from her second trip to the maternity ward—pled with tears on Willie's behalf. He got off with a suspended sentence. . . .

....

By his junior year of high school, Willie had dropped out, preferring to spend his days in the pool rooms of Harlem or out with the street hustlers. He was fascinated with their brand-new cars, glittering jewelry, and the ever-present attractive women.

He said to one of them one day, "Man! Nice stuff you've got here."

"Well, son," the man replied, "if you want what I got, you gotta do what I do." And thus came the teenager's first opportunities to work in the numbers racket, taking bets and collecting profits. He also began stealing cars. "In fact, I had master keys for all the brands: Ford, Dodge, Chevy," he admits.

One night while Willie was joyriding through Central Park, a squad car pulled up alongside. Willie floored it and, after screaming around a few curves, ran the car into a tree. He fled on foot. "Stop!" the officer cried, and threw a nightstick at him.

But once again Willie's court appearance proved anticlimactic. Of all coincidences, it turned out that the stolen car belonged to a friend of Willie's father, a fellow Mason! The man agreed not to press charges. . . .

At age seventeen Willie started experimenting with drugs. Of course, the hustlers had warned him, "If you're going to be good at this business, you can't use drugs. Don't be drinking, either. You gotta stay on your game in order to make money. People won't trust anybody who's messing around."

But Willie didn't follow the instructions. Acid, speed, cocaine, and especially heroin became common. In the "shooting galleries," he watched more than one guy die from a "hot shot"—a free dose from the dealer that was actually a punishment for snitching. The white powder looked like heroin, but it was really rat poison or battery acid.

"It seemed like I could not stop going to jail," Willie remembers. "I kept getting ninety days for this, sixty days for that: writing 'numbers' ... trespassing ... disorderly conduct ... shoplifting from Macy's. It seemed like the streets just kept calling my name. . . ."

Eventually, twenty-one counts of armed robbery led to a ten year sentence. As Willie talks about these days, it seems as if the jail times are so numerous they have begun to run together in his mind. Rikers Island here in the city, then upstate to Sing-Sing, then Greenhaven, then farther north to Clinton-Dannemora, forty miles from Canada, then Comstock (called "Gladiator School" at the time), and finally Walkhill.

One scary night in Clinton, however, is crystal-clear. A big, muscular inmate who was serving a life sentence with no hope of parole had begun befriending Willie, leaving candy, sodas, and cigarettes on his bunk. *How nice!* Willie thought.

But then one day the man announced, "Yo, I have some gambling debts to pay, and so I'm gonna need my money by tomorrow. You owe me forty-five dollars for all this stuff I've been providing you."

"Well," said Willie, quickly sizing up the situation, "I don't have it now, but I've got some money coming in the mail. I'll pay you as soon as it arrives."

"No, you didn't hear me," the man replied in a steely voice. "I said *tomorrow*. And if you don't have it, you're gonna be 'my kid.'"

The thought of providing forced homosexual service to this man terrified Willie. He stayed up all night, pacing back and forth in his six-by-eight cell, scared to death. The cellblock was buzzing with talk about what would go down next.

When the doors clanked open at five-thirty the next morning, Willie seized the initiative. Grabbing a mop bucket in the corridor, he bashed the guy over the head, opening a fountain of blood. Guards came running to tackle Willie, spraying him in the face with Mace and clubbing him into submission.

Inevitably, Willie was returned to court once again, this time on a charge of attempted murder. More time was added to his sentence. . . .

....

When Willie finally got out of prison in 1976, Elise and the two children were amazingly still waiting for him. The couple got married at last, over the strong protest of her family.

But the angry twenty-seven-year-old Willie was still out of control. Once when a man pulled a knife on him in the street, Willie grabbed the knife by the blade, slicing his finger badly. Elise came to see him in the hospital—and happened to show up just as a girlfriend named Renee was also making her call!

Willie refused to let his wife into the room. But the two women met in the lobby, and Elise asked to visit her home. She had heard about a new baby and wanted to investigate whether it belonged to Willie. Once she arrived, Elise was shocked to see an undeniable match for her husband's face.

The surgeons used a tendon from Willie's arm to repair his damaged finger. But not long afterward, while shooting dice, the other player said, "On that last throw, those dice didn't land right. I'm not paying up!" Willie smacked him— and the finger folded over. It is still bent to this day.

Willie's own father advised Elise, "You better get as much insurance on him as you can, because he isn't going to last long. . . ."

After the death of a daughter from diabetes, Willie became all the more violent. He stole $20,000 in drugs from a supplier, sold them, and used the money to enter the prostitution business.

Soon, however, the cash flow could not keep up with his expenses. "After all, you can smoke a thousand dollars' worth of crack in less than five hours—no problem," he admits. Before long, the drug supplier figured out who the culprit was and put out a contract on Willie's life. Willie was making a call at a public phone booth one day when, all of a sudden, bullets started flying. Willie twisted in first one direction and then the other as a 9mm bullet bounced off the phone and into his face. Passing through his tongue, the bullet split his jaw. Meanwhile, another bullet entered his shoulder from the back.

Ever the tough guy, Willie wanted to jump up and chase the attacker, who quickly climbed into a waiting station wagon and disappeared. Meanwhile, people began pouring out of the numbers parlors nearby. "Man, you got a hole in your face!" they shouted. "Stay still!"

Lying on the street, watching his blood run toward the gutter, Willie prayed for one of the few times in his life: "God, please don't let me go out like this."

When Elise, who had recently started attending our church, came to visit him in the hospital this time, she just stared. She showed no emotion at all.

"Aren't you going to cry?" Willie asked.

"No, I'm gonna pray for you. You need Jesus bad. . . ."

....

But Willie McLean was not yet ready to change. He met another girlfriend named Brigitte, who bore him two more children in the coming years. Brigitte's incensed mother tried to have him killed as well, but Willie managed to charm the designated gunmen into leaving him alone.

He did not fare so well with the police in Jamaica, Queens, however, after they photographed him from a rooftop making a drug sale. When he was brought before the grand jury, a cold sweat settled over him. *Everything's falling apart*, he told himself. *I'm headed back to jail for how long? Five years? More?*

The sentence this time was a year on Rikers Island plus five years' probation.

And that was the point when Elise finally managed to get her thirty-nine-year-old husband to our church. He had long pushed her away with excuses: no money for the offering, no clothes that would look right. But this time he gave in.

"The choir began singing that day," he recalls, "and I just opened up. My nose started running, and then I was actually crying!

"Then Pastor Cymbala started speaking. It seemed like, with all those people in the building, he was talking right to me. This guy somehow knew all my business!"

He turned to his wife. "Elise, did you tell him about me?"

"No—honestly, I didn't say anything."

Before Willie knew it, an invitation to come to Christ began. Willie found himself moving forward, tears beclouding his vision. At the front of the church he spread out his arms and cried, "O God—I just can't take it anymore. I can't go on...."

That was the beginning of a new life for this hardened criminal. "Even though I knew I was soon going back to jail," he says, "a ton of weight fell off my shoulders that day." He kept coming to church right up until it was time to report to Rikers Island.

During the year in prison, Willie asked God to free him from methadone—the drug replacement that counselors had been providing him for fifteen years to try to curb his appetite for heroin. In response to prayer, the detoxification process that should have taken years was completed in ten weeks. Soon Willie was out—and this time stayed clean.

Before another year passed, we had hired him to work in the maintenance department at the Brooklyn Tabernacle. He was clearly a new creation in Christ. Pastor Dan Iampaglia, one of our associates at the time, would say to Willie, "Brother, thank God your wife became a real Christian. Otherwise, she might have been tempted to blow you away a long time ago." (Elise worked for the federal government and was authorized to carry a .357 Magnum.)

"I know," Willie would respond. "I've put that woman through so much! I just thank God for Jesus. She couldn't have held on without the Lord."

Today Willie explains in his soft-spoken voice, "The Lord didn't just save me—he delivered me. He mended my marriage. He gave back my self-esteem. My son Michael, who would never speak to me, began to respect me. My father saw what God did for me and, after all these years, began to serve the Lord, too. My sister, who had been in prostitution, gave her heart to the Lord.

"My brother-in-law, who was taking advantage of his young stepdaughters, called me one day and was feeling so guilty he was ready to hang himself. But I began ministering to him. Today he's serving the Lord, singing in the Men's Chorus at the Brooklyn Tabernacle.

"God has turned my life inside out. He has blessed me and my family incredibly."

When we asked Willie to give his testimony from the pulpit of our church, he fought back tears as he began by reading a poignant passage of Scripture that summed up his amazing story:

> I thank Christ Jesus our Lord, who has given me strength, that he considered me faithful, appointing me to his service. Even though I was once a blasphemer and a persecutor and a violent man, I was shown mercy because I acted in ignorance and unbelief. The grace of our Lord was poured out on me abundantly, along with the faith and love that are in Christ Jesus.
>
> Here is a trustworthy saying that deserves full acceptance: Christ Jesus came into the world to save sinners—of whom I am the worst. But for that very reason I was shown mercy so that in me, the worst of sinners, Christ Jesus might display his unlimited patience as an example for those who would believe on him and receive eternal life. Now to the King eternal, immortal, invisible, the only God, be honor and glory for ever and ever. Amen (1 Timothy 1:12–17).

The power of the Holy Spirit got ahold of this giant of a man and stopped his self-destruction. And the same Spirit of God who turned Willie McLean to Christ and salvation has kept him clean and victorious ever since. Think of the power potential we have available to us through God's Word anointed by the Holy Spirit. Not just the Word only, nor an emphasis solely on the Spirit—we must have the Word and the Spirit together bringing blessing and salvation.

Let us pray for pastors everywhere, that a fresh, fiery anointing will come upon us as we speak from our pulpits. Let us ask God for preaching in our churches that brings the things of heaven down to earth with such power that our towns, cities, country, and world will be forever changed. Let us all join with that sincere man of God from another era who expressed his heart's desire in these words: "I long more and more to be filled with the Spirit, and to see my congregation moved and melted under the Word, as in great revival times, 'the place shaken where they are assembled together,' because the Lord has come in power."[4]

....

Lord, send a revival and let it begin in us, in our preaching, in our churches. But no matter how or where it begins, Lord, send a revival of the Holy Spirit among your people.

FIVE

Facing Heat

As we have already seen in the Acts 1 account of the upper room, spending time in communion with God is critical to our experience of the Spirit's power. It is not surprising that the book of Acts refers to a number of key prayer times in the life of the church. They are all instructive as to how the Christian church lived out its mission on earth.

On one occasion Peter and John were on the way to the temple to pray when something wonderful happened. The story begins this way:

> One day Peter and John were going up to the temple at the time of prayer—at three in the afternoon. Now a man crippled from birth was being carried to the temple gate called Beautiful, where he was put every day to beg from those going into the temple courts. When he saw Peter and John about to enter, he asked them for money. Peter looked straight at him, as did John. Then Peter said, "Look at us!" So the man gave them his attention, expecting to get something from them.
>
> Then Peter said, "Silver or gold I do not have, but what I have I give you. In the name of Jesus Christ of Nazareth, walk." Taking him by the right hand, he helped him up, and instantly the man's feet and ankles

became strong. He jumped to his feet and began to walk. Then he went with them into the temple courts, walking and jumping, and praising God (Acts 3:1–8).

The cripple at the Beautiful Gate was certainly not the only beggar that day; there may well have been others calling for Peter's and John's attention. But the Bible says that "Peter looked straight at him." Other translations say, "Peter, fastening his eyes upon him . . ." (KJV) or "Peter looked intently at the man" (Phillips).

I can tell you from a lifetime of living in New York City that most people try *not* to make eye contact with beggars and panhandlers. The defense mechanism is to pretend you don't even see these unfortunate people. You just keep walking steadily and get suddenly interested in the taxi in the street, the flashing billboard overhead—anything but the grizzled man collecting bottles, or the bag lady.

Peter responded exactly opposite to this. By the Spirit he perceived that God was about to do something for this individual. Peter did not feel drawn to everybody at the gate in some wholesale sort of way, but only to this particular man.

There was no indication that the cripple believed in Jesus the Messiah. He didn't ask Peter for prayer. He simply uttered the Jewish equivalent of "Buddy, can you spare some change?" like all the rest.

Yet Peter knew in his heart what to do—or rather he somehow knew what God was about to do. He initiated contact. "Look at us!" he declared.

WHAT DOES THE SPIRIT HAVE IN MIND?

This insight is something we need to recover today. Not very many of us expect God to give us these kinds of supernatural indications and leadings. The Holy Spirit may want to touch

someone with divine power and change his or her life forever—but he can't seem to find a channel to use, someone
whose spiritual antenna is pointed outward in a heavenly
direction and ready to obey God's prompting. The story in
Acts 3 is not hocus-pocus mysticism but a factual account of
what the Holy Spirit did through two yielded servants.

Too often we pray about problems in a mechanical way,
mouthing the same words over and over regardless of the
case. We would do far better if we waited on the Lord and
were sensitive to the mind of the Spirit about what to do,
what to say, and what *not* to say as we walk among needy
people, broken relationships, and other problems that come
our way. The same God who led Peter can lead us today.

Please notice that Peter did not declare healing to every
beggar at the temple gate that day, but only to one in particular. There is no basis anywhere in the New Testament for
mechanical, assembly-line operation of any spiritual gift
according to some whim of the Christian believer. Rather,
every indication is that we need to be open and obedient to
the moving and sovereign mind of the Holy Spirit.

Think of all we miss by not being in tune with the
Spirit's sensitive and yet powerful leadings. Within minutes
that day in Jerusalem, a crippled man was up on his feet,
jumping around and dancing for the first time in his life. And
isn't it remarkable that this did not happen *on the way home*
from a wonderful prayer meeting, after Peter and John had
been exalting the name of the Lord for two hours and were
on a great spiritual high? Instead, it happened as they "were
going *up to* the temple at the time of prayer—at three in the
afternoon" (Acts 3:1). They hadn't even been to the prayer
meeting yet, and still their hearts were so in tune with the
Spirit of God that they were instantly ready to cooperate with
what the Spirit wanted to do.

It is ironic that this pitiful man was found begging at the temple gate called *Beautiful*. The inner-city setting where Carol and I minister has a lot of filth and ugliness on all sides. Things are not very beautiful here. But outside of the 'hood there are loads of crippled people all across America, even some in beautiful settings. They are not crippled physically but are beggars of another kind. They have tasted material success, financial security, and physical pleasures—but are still empty, with nobody home in their souls. May God raise up an army to speak words of healing and deliverance to these "other cripples."

This man's sudden walking and jumping and leaping were fairly dramatic evidence that the name of Jesus had power. A crowd gathered in wonderment—the second crowd in church history to be evangelized. Again, notice what brought them together: *a manifestation of the Spirit's power through the believers,* just as on the Day of Pentecost. Not the same demonstration, to be sure, but something that made people ask, "How did this happen?"

A BOLD EXPLANATION

Peter begins to speak, again with a healthy portion of boldness. "You disowned the Holy and Righteous One," he says in Acts 3:14. Well, look who's talking! Hadn't Peter done his own disowning of Christ around the campfire a few weeks previous? Yet all that is in the past now, thanks to the power of the blood of Jesus and the empowerment of the Holy Spirit in Peter's life. He is not wallowing in self-condemnation. He knows that what God forgives, God also forgets, so Peter courageously addresses the crowd.

No doubt some of his listeners had been among the mob in Pilate's court shouting, "Crucify him! Crucify him!" You would think that Peter would be a little more diplomatic here. But the last thing on his mind is what these folks *want* to hear. He is fearless to declare what they *need* to hear. Their reaction to the Word of God is not his business—only to be faithful to his calling as a spokesperson for Christ.

Peter says, "By faith in the name of Jesus, this man whom you see and know was made strong. It is Jesus' name and the faith that comes through him that has given this complete healing to him, as you can all see" (v. 16). The faith was obviously not in the man. It was in the hearts of Peter and John. This was not just a mental affirmation of certain facts concerning the life of Jesus. Nor was it a parroting of some mantra of "I believe, I believe, you are healed, you are healed." This was a Spirit-born faith that God gave to Peter, tailored exactly to the unique situation he faced that day.

> **Whatever God *calls* us to do, he will also be faithful to *equip* us to do.**

We can rest assured today that whatever God *calls* us to do, he will also be faithful to *equip* us to do. Remember that "God, who has called you into fellowship with his Son Jesus Christ our Lord, is faithful" (1 Corinthians 1:9). We are co-laborers with Christ through the Holy Spirit's work in and through us.

Peter's sermon produced a second wave of converts that day, so that the church grew to some 5,000.

BACKLASH

But at the same moment, persecution struck. We read in Acts 4:1–3 that before Peter and John could hardly turn around, they got "busted." They ended up spending the night in jail.

What was it that triggered the arrest? The priests and Sadducees "were greatly disturbed because the apostles were . . .

proclaiming in Jesus the resurrection of the dead" (v. 2). If Peter had just softened his message to something more palatable ... maybe a little sermonette on kosher food, or how beautiful the temple looked that day ... he could have stayed out of trouble. But that is not God's way.

It is the way of people devoid of faith in the Holy Spirit's power. They are always cleverly figuring out what will "work" to keep the crowd and remain popular. This is one component of the disastrous "church growth" movement. Nowhere does God tell us to have large churches, or that growth in numbers is a sign that all is well. What he does call for is for us to do *his* work in *his* way by preaching *his* Word under *his* power for *his* glory. I believe that if by his grace we do that, "numbers" will come—not as a goal but as a by-product of God's blessing.

Let us remember that there has always been persecution in one form or another. Just as Satan tried to kill the baby Jesus in Bethlehem, here we see him going after the infant church. Sometimes persecution is overt and violent; at other times it is more subtle.

It is really embarrassing for us to read this story in light of what we call "problems," what we complain about. Compared with what happened to the apostles in Acts 4, we have a walk in the park. We still have the freedom to meet, to preach, to hand out Christian literature. Yet we blame the environment for our powerlessness rather than facing our spiritual condition. We talk endlessly about how godless the country is becoming when the only answer to the situation is for us, the church, to return to our spiritual birthright as a powerful community in Jesus Christ.

How did God's people respond to genuine intimidation and persecution?

At the apostles' arraignment the next morning before the Jewish power structure, including the high priest, there were very few opening pleasantries. The first question was hurled straight into their faces: "By what power or what name did you do this?" (v. 7).

Notice how the writer, Luke, sets up the scene in verse 8: "Then Peter, *filled with the Holy Spirit*, said to them...." Why do you think Luke inserted that extra clause? If Peter and the others had been categorically and permanently filled with the Spirit back in the upper room, why bring it up here? If Spirit infilling is just a standard part of Christianity for all believers, why this peculiar mention? It would be like writing, "Then Peter, *who was breathing*, said to them...."

Apparently Luke felt there was something noteworthy here that needed to be pointed out. Peter was not just standing up as a former fisherman to try and answer his inquisitors as best he could in himself. He wasn't just going to quote something he had heard from Jesus during his three years of training. Instead, he was a man under the control and anointing of the Spirit of God himself! We marvel once again at the thought: It was Peter, sure enough, a man with frailties and weaknesses like all of us—but it wasn't exactly Peter alone. It was "Peter, filled with the Holy Spirit," so that this court didn't really understand what it was up against.

Thank God for these special enduements of power for critical moments in life. We need to trust God for these when we hit our own difficulties and challenges. We must always remember that "trials are the opening of channels for more grace."[1]

The longer Peter talked, the more amazed the dignitaries became. "When they saw the courage of Peter and John and realized that they were unschooled, ordinary men, they were astonished" (Acts 4:13). These fellows certainly weren't eloquent. Perhaps their sandals even had a little leftover smell of fish bait. Peter was, as we would say in New York, "not even close." How ludicrous for these know-nothings to represent

themselves as religious leaders! They were Galileans, bump-
kins, hayseeds. What a joke to the proud Sanhedrin and its
vaunted traditions.

Yet these men showed no fear, no intimidation before the
highest governing body in Judaism. Didn't they understand
that this council had arranged the
crucifixion of Jesus and could easily
do it again to his followers?

Yes, they understood. But the
power of the Holy Spirit made them
fearless.

A lot of us today would do well to
hear again what the aged Paul, sitting
on death row in a Roman dungeon,
wrote to the young Timothy: "God
did not give us a spirit of timidity, but
a spirit of power, of love and of self-
discipline" (2 Timothy 1:7). We must never be intimidated
by what the devil tries to do, whether by striking out at us as
individuals, or at the local church, or at the Body of Christ as
a whole. We must instead trust the Holy Spirit to give us the
words to speak, and to do so with boldness.

> These fellows certainly weren't eloquent. Perhaps their sandals even had a little leftover smell of fish bait. Peter was, as we would say in New York, "not even close."

LIVING EVIDENCE

The Sanhedrin, of course, had a slight problem. "Since they
could see the man who had been healed standing there with
them, there was nothing they could say" (Acts 4:14). This is
our need today—for clear examples of the power of God.
Whether it is a crack addict who has been set free, a child
who has been healed, a homosexual who has been turned
around, or a hedonist who has changed—there's something
irrefutable about a brand-new life filled with peace and joy

from the Holy Spirit. We need living arguments, trophies of God's grace, to refute our critics. The Word of God is our message, as it was Peter's. Can't God give us living testimonies in order to show the world that "Jesus Christ is the same yesterday and today and forever" (Hebrews 13:8)?

Sometimes when the Brooklyn Tabernacle Choir goes out to sing, we make time between songs for members to tell their personal stories. My wife, Carol, the director, wants to remind audiences that the Jesus of whom the choir is singing is still mighty to save. On more than one occasion, Pam Peña—the wife of one of our associate pastors—has shared how the Lord delivered her from a terrible eating disorder. Raised in a churchgoing home in the New Jersey suburbs, she was an emotionally needy teenager who lacked self-confidence and felt worthless. The opinion of her peers was all-important.

This pretty young woman with short brown hair recalls for the audience how, to please her friends, she began cutting school, drinking, and smoking. At age sixteen she found herself pregnant. Her boyfriend rejected her, and she was devastated. Feeling all alone, she quickly obtained an abortion.

In the aftermath of this, she told herself, *Maybe if I turn to God and try harder to do the right thing, he will accept me.* She didn't realize that she was now trying to win God's approval through her own efforts. As time went on, these efforts left her empty. She remained insecure about who she was and became obsessed with the weight she had gained.

Her first two years at a Christian college saw compulsive dieting and vigorous exercise—to the point that friends began to comment. Pam decided she had better eat to please them, but would then retreat to the bathroom to purge the food from her stomach. She felt disillusioned, not comprehending the grace of God that welcomed her just as she was.

By the end of her sophomore year she was weak and thin from bingeing and purging up to five times a day.

She dropped out of college, went home to New Jersey, and decided not even to try to serve God anymore. This time she fled to a secular college, Virginia Tech, where her life spun further out of control. Someone introduced her to cocaine, which among other things is a powerful appetite suppressant. She quickly became addicted.

The next three years were a downward spiral of food abuse compounded by cocaine. At a party one desperate New Year's Eve, she went into the host family's bathroom and cleaned out the medicine chest of every pill she could find, putting them into her purse. At home the next day, she swallowed them all, then lay down to die.

While waiting, she called a college friend—and that fortunately led to her rescue. But even six weeks in a residential treatment program couldn't break her compulsion over food. Another patient there, in fact, informed her one day of the best place in the area to buy cocaine! Pam promptly put the tip to use when she got out.

In about a year, she attempted suicide a second time. She deliberately drove onto a major highway with her eyes closed and was hit by a bus. The crash was horrific, demolishing her car. Pam had to be pried out of the vehicle—but amazingly walked away unscathed. All this time, her parents and their church family were earnestly praying that God would somehow rescue Pam from herself.

Finally, while living with a boyfriend who was drug-free, Pam was holding down two waitress jobs, the second one for the sole purpose of financing her cocaine purchases behind the boyfriend's back. The relationship was understandably tense. One morning, while driving to a country club in Wayne, New Jersey, to work the lunch shift, she said to herself, "Either this guy's going to catch me doing drugs and he'll react violently, or else I'm going to try to take my life again. In fact ... how can I do it and really make it work this time?"

And in that moment, at the end of her rope, she began to cry out to the Lord. Sobbing so hard that no sound would come from her throat, her soul nevertheless was shouting, *O God, I want to live!*

There on the Hamburg Turnpike, "the love of God came into the car," she remembers. "I finally gave up trying to be loved by people. I quit striving for approval. I saw my self-deception.

"The Lord reminded me of my walk to a tent meeting altar back at age five, and it was like he said, 'I have always loved you.' Finally I saw with my spiritual eyes what I had been missing. I seemed to fall into God's arms, saying, 'I give up. I *will* believe that you love me.'"

Pam quit the waitressing job immediately. She never touched cocaine again. Cigarettes were dropped within weeks. And God the Holy Spirit went to work on the eating disorder. Over the next two years, without any psychotherapy or seminars, Pam gradually stopped the harmful behavior. During the process, when difficult moments came, God seemed to assure her that he had her by the hand and would pull her completely from the pit where she had lived for so long.

"I went back to church and began devouring the Word of God. The truth was setting me free from my bondage and deception. I came to understand that my eating habits were a form of sin, because my body was not really my own. I didn't have the right to binge and purge. The Lord brought me to repentance for that. He was also renewing my mind day by day.

"I had to trust the Lord that if I ate food and kept it down, I wouldn't gain weight—or if I did, he would enable me to deal with that situation. Little by little the Holy Spirit taught me how to eat."

During this time Pam met and married Alex, who was a good influence in spiritual things. Their first child was born entirely healthy in spite of all that Pam had done to her body. Since then, two more beautiful children have come to the family.

As she gives her testimony, Pam often tells about one particular mealtime: Thanksgiving 1988. Holidays can be the worst nightmare for a bulimic person. "I sat down at the big table with all the other relatives, had Thanksgiving dinner—and even accepted some dessert. As I was eating it, the Holy Spirit seemed to whisper in my ear, *You're fine. It's finally over.*

"I stood up from the table and went upstairs to a quiet room. There I began to sob and thank God. Since that day more than ten years ago, there has been no bingeing or purging—not even the temptation to do so. At times when I've felt fully 'stuffed' after a meal, I've still had no urge to head for the bathroom. It has been a complete deliverance. I've been set free to trust God and his grace."

Once after Pam spoke in a large Dallas church, God used her story to bring a woman with a similar disorder into freedom and deliverance. But do you know what is curious? She has also had Christian people in other places come up afterward to say, "That's impossible. We can't believe that actually happened to you."

Well, the facts are that God performed a miracle in the life of Pam Peña. Today she is a wonderful servant of the Lord who brings others into freedom in our church. And it all happened, not through human strategies, but rather through the gracious influence of the Holy Spirit.

What is the success rate of secular psychiatry today? How effective are government drug-treatment programs?

The marvelous thing about Teen Challenge, started by my friend David Wilkerson, is that its Christ-centered message has helped young men and women to get free from drugs more effectively than many other programs; government studies have even documented this. The Spirit's power is greater than even the seductive lure of heroin and cocaine.

FIGHT, FLEE, OR . . . ?

In spite of the evidence of good being done, the Sanhedrin could not afford to cave in to Peter and John. They broke for an executive session and then "called them in again and commanded them not to speak or teach *at all* in the name of Jesus" (Acts 4:18). Peter replied that such a restriction was not really going to work, which led to "further threats" (v. 21) before the proceeding ended.

What were the apostles' options at this point? I see at least three:

1. The church, with 5,000 members or more, could flex its collective muscle. They could mount a public demonstration, marching around the halls of government in protest. "After all," they could say, "we're not just a ragtag bunch of twelve disciples anymore. We are a voting bloc to be reckoned with. We demand our rights. You're going to have to give us a fair shake." That would have been—as it is now—a dead-end approach to a hostile spiritual environment.

2. They could have said, "Wait a minute—we had a great visitation from God back in the upper room. There was a great wind, tongues of fire, and speaking in other languages. Because of that, we're invincible. We can take on anybody. Come on, guys!—let's keep quoting the promises: 'The Lord is my Shepherd, I shall not want.' 'I will never leave you nor forsake you.' Our faith confession will make this whole mess go away."

3. They could have just given up. Peter could have said, "You can't fight city hall, you know. These people definitely have the connections with Rome to kill us. We'd better get out of town and go back to fishing. God is omnipotent and sovereign anyway, so why does he need us risking our necks?"

The apostles chose none of these. They didn't start a political action committee, they didn't rely on past spiritual experience, and they didn't throw in the towel. Instead, they went to a prayer meeting. The Bible says, "They raised their voices together in prayer to God" (v. 24). You would, too, if your life was being threatened! Even if it wasn't your tradition to practice collective prayer, you would probably call out in desperation. This was a passionate cry for help.

> The apostles didn't start a political action committee, they didn't rely on past spiritual experience, and they didn't throw in the towel. Instead, they went to a prayer meeting.

No matter what you or I have been taught, no matter what church setting we have experienced, we see that prayer in the early church was apparently a very vocal, very earnest thing. But then again, David had showed much the same emotion: "I cried out to God for help; I cried out to God to hear me. When I was in distress, I sought the Lord; at night I stretched out untiring hands" (Psalm 77:1–2). So this kind of praying was not new to God's people.

Too many times when we are under stress or opposition, we do everything but call a prayer meeting. We try to pull political levers, we hold strategy sessions, we "claim the promises" in a rote sort of way instead of praying them biblically. But God said we could "receive mercy and find grace to help us in our time of need." Where? At "the throne of grace" (Hebrews 4:16).

Have we forgotten Paul's instruction to Timothy? "I urge, then, *first of all*, that requests, prayers, intercession and thanksgiving be made for everyone. . . . This is good, and pleases God our Savior. . . . I want men everywhere to lift up holy hands in prayer, without anger or disputing" (1 Timothy 2:1, 3, 8). Paul could think of nothing more important to do, nothing that should go onto the schedule ahead of prayer.

This group in Jerusalem cried out to the Lord for him to "enable your servants to speak your word with great boldness" (Acts 4:29). In response, "the place where they were meeting was shaken," as in an earthquake. There was no doubt that they had made contact with heaven. The story closes with this sentence: "And they were all filled with the Holy Spirit and spoke the word of God boldly" (v. 31).

> We need continual infillings of the Spirit to meet the strong, ungodly tendencies of the age.

Now wait a minute! Hadn't they been filled with the Holy Spirit back on the Day of Pentecost? What is this new filling all about?

This proves that we can't live off what God did in our lives last week, last month, or last year. We need continual infillings of the Spirit to meet the strong, ungodly tendencies of the age. There must be deeper enduements of power to meet deeper challenges. The greater the onslaught and the more evil the tactics that Satan comes up with, the more God's Spirit must be entreated to come and prepare us for battle. This is why D. L. Moody (see the prologue) called his convocation in 1880 for people to come and seek God for the fresh infilling of the Spirit's power that was so evidently needed.

John Wesley, founder of the Methodist movement, preached a whole sermon in 1744 on Acts 4:31—to an audience at his alma mater, Oxford University, no less. It was a ringing call to let the Holy Spirit have his way. He barraged his listeners with a volley of hard-hitting questions about their spiritual lassitude, rising near the end to this climax:

> How few of you spend, from one week to another, a single hour in private prayer! How few have any thought of God in the general tenor of your conversation! Who of you is, in any degree, acquainted with the work of his Spirit, his supernatural work in the souls of men? Can you bear, unless now and then, in a church, any talk of the Holy Ghost? Would you not take it for granted, if one began such a conversation, that it was either hypocrisy or enthusiasm? In the name of the Lord God Almighty, I ask, What religion are you of?[2]

That is a very interesting question for us here at the beginning of the twenty-first century. *What religion are we of?* I believe there is a growing number of Christians across the land who are hungry for the religion of the Bible, the Christianity of the New Testament in all its spiritual splendor. They are not satisfied by the contemporary American church culture nor by the fruit it is producing. While the evil tide of the world, the flesh, and the devil is rising to flood stage, the Lord is raising up a godly standard against it—men and women whose hearts cry out with the psalmist:

> O God, you are my God,
>   earnestly I seek you;
> my soul thirsts for you,
>   my body longs for you,
> in a dry and weary land
>   where there is no water.

I have seen you in the sanctuary
    and beheld your power and your glory.
Because your love is better than life,
    my lips will glorify you.
I will praise you as long as I live,
    and in your name I will lift up my hands.
My soul will be satisfied as with the richest of foods;
    with singing lips my mouth will praise you (Psalm
    63:1–5).

SIX

A House United

IN 1858, A TALL, gangly man stood up in Springfield, Illinois, to accept his party's nomination for U.S. senator. America was at that moment being ripped apart by fierce debate over the peculiar institution of slavery. Who would carry the day—the slaveholders or the abolitionists? Could a country survive half slave and half free?

In his acceptance speech Abraham Lincoln made a prophetic declaration. Quoting Jesus, he insisted, "A house divided against itself cannot stand." In other words, there was no way to dodge this issue: America must choose one or the other.

Lincoln's speech gained exposure in newspapers back east, and although he lost the election that November, he began to influence the greater argument across the nation. That is why two years later he was quickly catapulted into the office of president. The bloody Civil War fulfilled his prediction. More people died in that conflict than in all of the nation's other wars put together. Through it all, Lincoln became one of America's most courageous national heroes.

ONE HEART AND MIND

This principle of unity and its paramount importance was imparted to the early church through the person and work of the Spirit of God. A lot more than anointed preaching and powerful evangelism was going on, for the Holy Spirit produced something wonderful, as described in Acts 4:32: "All the believers were one in heart and mind." This unity was not organized by the apostles, who had shown their own flurries of disunity and dissension while following Jesus of Nazareth. Rather, it was God-produced, love-constructed, and Spirit-born.

The disunity and division that prevail today are holding back the work of God. As a result, millions of unbelievers are getting a distorted view of the Body of Christ.

It is sad but true that Christian marriages often end up divided, with divorce rates that are no better than American society at large. Church boards are fighting with their pastors. Church staff members are competitive and jealous of one another. Choirs are riddled by gossip and division.

A minister of music told me once that he hadn't spoken a word to his senior pastor in four months because of the tension between them. But as long as he kept producing two songs for each Sunday service, that would be just fine.

"You must have some really glorious services," I said, shaking my head. How could God bless in that kind of environment?

This is a crucial question before us, for what good are even the gifts of the Holy Spirit if people continue hassling each other? What is the benefit of great preaching if the listeners snub one other on the way out the door?

Jesus said unity is paramount, and we need to listen to him again very closely: "A new *command* I give you: Love one another. As I have loved you, so you *must* love one another" (John 13:34). Of course, this is not humanly possible; it throws us upon the power of the Holy Spirit, because how in the world could we by ourselves love other Christians as Jesus loved us?! No pastor can instill divine love in a congregation by merely teaching about it; it must be "poured out ... into our hearts by the Holy Spirit, whom he has given us" (Romans 5:5).

Jesus insisted, "All men will know that you are my disciples if you love one another" (John 13:35). This is the sign that we really belong to him—not that we can quote the Bible, not that we're Calvinist or Arminian, not whether we're Baptist or Nazarene, Presbyterian or Pentecostal. The acid test for a real Christian experience is our love for one another. Think of it!

But how woefully little of that do we see today. Ministers often refuse to assist or even fellowship with other ministers of a different denomination. Good news about a given church is discounted by other Christians, or received with skepticism. On the other hand, bad news, such as a scandal, is welcomed with a smirk that says, "I always knew there was something not quite right about those folks...."

We have sometimes made honest attempts to *teach* love in the Body of Christ—but how do you teach something that is the very essence of God? We can only go deeper in love as we go deeper with the Lord. In the simple words of 1 John 4:16, "God *is* love."

Jesus prayed for all his people to become one, just as he and his Father are one. But look around at our fragmentation. We talk about "evangelical" churches, "charismatic" churches, "Baptist" churches, and "Lutheran" churches. The problem is, God recognizes none of these artificial labels. He didn't think them up in the first place, and he doesn't use them now. In the words of Ephesians 4:4–6, there is only "one body and one Spirit ... one Lord, one faith, one baptism; one God and Father of all." Note: God has only *one* body, *one* family, made up of all us Christians. There are no subgroups within it as far as he is concerned.

I have a strong suspicion that God does not appreciate those who fragment his family. Carol and I have three children and five grandchildren, and if someone tried to drive a wedge between us or start a feud of some kind, we would quickly get upset. The same is true in the spiritual family. It is a very serious offense, which is why Paul wrote, "I urge you, brothers, to watch out for those who cause divisions and put obstacles in your way that are contrary to the teaching you have learned. Keep away from them. For such people are not serving our Lord Christ, but their own appetites" (Romans 16:17–18).

> I have a strong suspicion that God does not appreciate those who fragment his family.

When was the last time, if ever, that you saw a church member disciplined for causing division among believers? If someone who professes Christ was caught dabbling in witchcraft or practicing adultery, we would all cry for some kind of church action. But divisive, gossiping people go right on attending our churches and sometimes even hold leadership positions. We never address their ugly sin and destructiveness because we are so used to it.

Paul the apostle told the Corinthians—who were preoccupied with spiritual gifts, by the way—that their divisions were a sign of carnality and immaturity. This shows that sensational phenomena do not automatically prove spiritual maturity. Only love gives us those credentials. The greatest Christian in my church or yours is the person most filled with the love of God.

DIVIDED WE FALL

The biblical account that inspired Abraham Lincoln goes like this:

The teachers of the law who came down from Jerusalem said, "He is possessed by Beelzebub! By the prince of demons he is driving out demons."

So Jesus called them and spoke to them in parables: "How can Satan drive out Satan? If a kingdom is divided against itself, that kingdom cannot stand. If a house is divided against itself, that house cannot stand. And if Satan opposes himself and is divided, he cannot stand; his end has come" (Mark 3:22–26).

Satan, of course, is too smart to let his troops get divided against each other. They stay in line and always keep the main goal in mind. Isn't it sad that we the church, by contrast, are not that wise?

What the teachers of the law proposed—that Jesus was overcoming the powers of darkness through some kind of secret alliance with them—was not only illogical but highly insulting to the Son of God. Jesus could well have replied, "Excuse me, but do you know who I am? Are you aware that I was sent here by my Father, the God of the universe, on a divine mission? When I arrived in Bethlehem's manger, I had just left the streets of gold. My true home is as far from Satan's headquarters as you can imagine."

Jesus didn't say that at all. He totally bypassed the personal vindication in order to make a spiritual point: *Any kingdom divided against itself—even Satan's—is doomed.* If the devil were in a civil war and had dissension in his ranks, his end would eventually come. But it was fairly obvious in Jesus' day that Satan was in business. And here today, two thousand years later, he is still in business and doing quite well.

Meanwhile, we have countless local churches divided against themselves, yet thinking God can somehow bless them. They don't understand that division quickly grieves the gentle Holy Spirit and undermines every work of grace. It doesn't matter whether the pastor preaches orthodox doctrine straight from the Bible. It doesn't matter whether he is a man of prayer. Unless division, strife, slander, and fighting are conquered, all his labor is in vain. Division causes a treadmill effect: We are busy expending energy to move ahead, but we go nowhere in the end. At the same time that we beckon the Spirit to "come" through our praying and preaching, our slander, backbiting, and division yell at him to "go away." This can persist for decades with congregations floating aimlessly, dead in the water.

Everywhere I travel, it seems, I hear new war stories about divided church boards, factions within congregations, and staff personnel clashing over the silliest of things. In such an atmosphere, God's Spirit can never bless, since he is the Spirit of peace.

Frank Bartleman, a Christian writer in the early part of the twentieth century, wrote, "The doctor looks at the tongue first thing. Have you been speaking evil? That denotes a bad heart. Every radical movement for God has ultimately failed on the test of love."

No pastoral staff that is fractured will experience God's best upon its work. That is why I often advise senior pastors to hire according to spirit first and talent second. The most gifted musicians or youth workers in the nation are unlikely to bring a blessing to a congregation if they carry strife and gossip and innuendo. What good is a secretarial whiz if she causes division among the staff?

Remember, we are *Christ's* church, not Apple Computer or AT&T. In the church, spiritual principles are foremost. I have seen a lot of "sharp" people turn out to be so sharp they cut and wound all kinds of people, and it is often difficult to stop the bleeding.

CHOIRS OFF KEY

No choir divided against itself can stand. A choir has to have the anointing of God's Spirit, because God does not bless pieces of sheet music; God blesses and uses human beings. If a soloist has a great voice but is living a sinful double life, there is little hope that God will anoint that person's song with power even if the lyrics are correct and the voice is magnificent. The soloist is grieving the Holy Spirit. The same is true when backbiting and jealousy seep into the life of a choir. The human vessels can taint and discolor the pure message of God's truth.

When my wife goes to a music conference and is asked, "Carol, what would you say is the key to music being a ministry instead of a performance?" she will respond, "It's not whether the tenors are on their note, or the orchestration is well done, or the microphones are properly placed. The main question before God is *who is singing*. He can only bless people who are *in tune* (to use a musical phrase) with him and with one another.

"That is why we begin every choir practice with a season of prayer. We do our best to seek the Lord and his blessing. The choir's ability to minister can never be better than their spiritual tone."

Crack cocaine, alcohol, and sexual temptation have slain their thousands, but bickering, quarreling, and criticism in the church have slain their ten thousands. No wonder the heart-attack rate for ordained ministers is off the charts. I can assure you that their worst strain comes not from sermon preparation but from dealing with all the carnality, tension, division, and politics within the ranks.

> **Crack cocaine, alcohol, and sexual temptation have slain their thousands, but bickering, quarreling, and criticism in the church have slain their ten thousands.**

Let us pray that God will raise up more voices led by the Spirit to bring this issue out into the open. One of the Apostolic Fathers, Ignatius of Antioch, wrote about a confrontation some seventy to eighty years after the time of Christ:

> When I visited your church at Philadelphia [a city some 100 miles inland from Ephesus] there was a faction in the church that was undermining the authority of the church's leadership and questioning their decisions. *Now God is my witness that I knew nothing about this at all.* No one had told me about it, and no rumor had reached my ears.
>
> So when I stood up to prophesy, and shouted in a loud voice, "Give more respect to your bishop, your elders and your deacons!" it was the Holy Spirit in me who was speaking. Although I know some of you think I had been told in advance of the divisions in Philadelphia, and spoke from knowledge, the absolute truth is that this was the voice of God alone.
>
> So remember and obey the other things I said as well: "Keep your bodies as temples of God. Love unity. Shun divisions."[1]

Not only is the Christian church in jeopardy from dissension, but so also is the Christian home. No husband and wife divided against each other can stand. Leaders from two different denominations recently admitted to me that their *ministerial* divorce rates are at all-time highs. Most times the trouble begins with a divisive wall, unforgiveness, resentment, and bitterness. It ends up bringing shame, upheaval, and heartache to children as well as congregations.

For our own lives as well, listen to David's prayer in Psalm 86:11: "Give me an undivided heart, that I may fear your name." David knew that no person divided on the inside can stand spiritually. We know from scandals in recent years that some who preached the gospel—who knew what is right but still got divided on the inside and gave loose rein to the flesh—ended up in a horrible mess. It all began with a divided heart that gave place for Satan to work further evil.

BEYOND COLOR

We need congregations to meet together in prayer with the same burden Paul expressed in Romans 15:5–6. "May the God who gives endurance and encouragement *give you a spirit of unity among yourselves* as you follow Christ Jesus, so that *with one heart and mouth* you may glorify the God and Father of our Lord Jesus Christ." We must cry out to the Holy Spirit to come do this among us.

Dr. Martin Luther King Jr. was the one who said back in the 1960s, "Eleven o'clock on Sunday morning is the most segregated hour of the week." Here we are, forty years later, and that is still true. All across America, people do drugs interracially, they go to work interracially, they do prison time together, they cheer together for their favorite sports team, they mingle freely in the parks and on buses—but when Sunday morning comes, everybody splits up. Whites are here, blacks are over there, Hispanics and Asians are elsewhere, while we all sing "Love Lifted Me." Something is seriously wrong with this picture.

> Unless the church doors arc lovingly open to everyone, regardless of color and ethnic background, they are not fully open to the Holy Spirit.

Believers across the United States often rationalize this racism and prejudice, but it's a cover-up, and even non-Christians see through it. I wonder how many minority people have been turned off to Jesus and the love of God because they never felt love from Christians they know. And almost everyone knows by now that the platitude of "homogeneous churches grow fastest" is just code language for racial prejudice. It is also not found in the Bible. The goal of Scripture is not fast-growing churches but rather congregations that please God. We might very well grow in numbers by appealing to such nasty impulses, but all of it sickens the heart of God. Unless the church doors are lovingly open to everyone, regardless of color and ethnic background, they are not fully open to the Holy Spirit.

Have we forgotten that we are serving the God who brought Jew and Gentile together in the book of Acts? These groups had such strong hatred against each other that our racial problems today seem tame in comparison. Yet there was not a church for Jews and a different church for Gentiles. God broke all that down through the unity of the Spirit.

In one church I visited, a leading elder told me, to my horror, that they had earmarked a certain adult Sunday school class just for minorities! And we wonder why the world doesn't believe our message? I have also experienced firsthand in New York City that minority churches often hold prejudice and resentment against whites, which is just as nasty. I'm afraid the landscape is littered with "cultural churches"—white, black, etc.—with few spiritual congregations such as we find in the Word of God.

Any church that wants to know the fullness of God's power and blessing, a continual harvest of souls, good discipleship, and strong prayer meetings must deal with the division in its midst. It must *"make every effort* to keep the unity of the Spirit through the bond of peace" (Ephesians 4:3). Yes, the Spirit is about power, but he is also about unity and love. He insists that we repent of racism and division of every kind.

When Ken Landis shows up for the Friday night choir practice at our church, he has been driving for two and a half hours just to get there. Leaving his job as a carpenter in the small eastern Pennsylvania town of Perkasie by mid-afternoon, he has crossed the entire state of New Jersey for a one-way trip of 110 miles and paid seven dollars in bridge or tunnel tolls—all for the privilege of singing with people who are mostly not of his color. He won't get home again until one o'clock Saturday morning.

> Yes, the Spirit is about power, but he is also about unity and love. He insists that we repent of racism and division of every kind.

Why would this gentle, fifty-three-year-old, self-described "country boy" do such an outlandish thing? And why would he make the trip all over again on Sunday for the church services?

It makes no sense until you hear Ken's story. For more than twenty years he lived a predictable life in a small town, working with his hands to support his wife and five children, going to church and being an average Christian. Only when his marriage came apart and his wife moved out to live with a man she had met while country line dancing was he shaken to the core.

For the previous year he had been playing cassettes of our choir while working or driving in his truck, and now, in his pain, he decided one September day to travel all the way into Brooklyn to go to church. Not knowing the city at all, he had to ask AAA for directions. Once he arrived, found a parking place on the street, and entered the building, he couldn't help noticing that white faces like his were hardly the majority.

"But God was drawing me. I could sense the Lord was here.

"I'd always been proud to be white. I looked down on other races. Now here I was, sitting in a pew with all kinds of people who were so in love with God that they reached out to me. They befriended me and cared about me.

"Every time I turned around, it seemed like someone was praying for me. Back in my home church, people had politely said, 'We'll pray for you, Ken,' shook my hand—and then headed out the door. Here were total strangers actually doing it. And through all this, God was loving me and drawing me to himself.

"It just made me hungry for a closer walk with the Lord."

The next Sunday, Ken Landis made the long trip again to offset the pain of his loneliness. The choir's music kept ministering to him at low times when he didn't want to go on living. One Thursday night he found himself wandering around K-Mart looking for a length of hose to hook up to his truck's exhaust pipe so he could commit suicide. But he eventually walked out of the store without making the purchase. That Sunday, he was back at the Brooklyn Tabernacle.

"At the end of the message that day," he remembers, "Pastor Cymbala said, 'Some of you here today have serious problems, and if you don't give them over to God, they're going to destroy you.' I knew that was me. I went forward for prayer.

"I felt a hand on my shoulder, interceding for me. When I turned around, it was a choir member from Haiti. I got to know him later—Billy Strackman. Before I could return to my pew only ten rows back, my agony had started to lift. The peace of God came down into my soul. He gave me a forgiveness for my wife and even for the guy she's with, so I could pray for them with a clean heart."

The next January, when choir tryouts were announced, a woman asked Ken if he was going to sign up. "Oh, I'd love to, but I could never make it," he replied.

"Brother," she said, pointing her finger at him, "this choir is not just about singing. It's about ministry."

Today Ken is one of a dozen or so appointed leaders in the choir. He sings in at least two services every Sunday, which means leaving home at nine in the morning and getting back at midnight. He calls it "the shortest day of my week."

"The thing that had to be broken in my life was my self-will. Now I'm just living for Jesus, standing in the gap for my kids, my grandkids, and even my wife. I've never been happier as a Christian."

Ken Landis is a man whose spiritual life was transformed by Christ revealing himself in a colorblind love that comes only from the Spirit of God.

We have seen the same thing happen in the other direction, as black people steeped in racial bitterness have been softened by the Spirit of Christ. Some of them have initially had problems with the idea of a white senior pastor and have said, "What is this—am I going to humiliate myself by attending a church pastored by 'the man'?" But soon the spotlight shifts off of human color and onto the God of all grace, who brings us together at his feet. Anyway, I'm white only on the outside, as others are black or brown. On the inside, we are all the same, with needs that only Jesus Christ can meet.

Let me repeat: If the doors of the church are not open to everyone, they will never be fully open to the Holy Spirit. God is not the God of a black church or a white church. It won't be that way in heaven. If people here on earth don't want to be with those of another race, why would God ruin their eternity by bringing them into a place with those "from every nation, tribe, people and language,

> If people here on earth don't want to be with those of another race, why would God ruin their eternity by bringing them into a place with those "from every nation, tribe, people and language"?

standing before the throne and in front of the Lamb" (Revelation 7:9)?

Yes, we need an enduement of power from on high, but we also need a fresh baptism of God's love. The Lord is not going to use angels or a voice from the clouds in heaven to spread his message. He has chosen to let us be his hand extended. But his heart is one of infinite tender compassion to all humanity, for "God does not show favoritism" (Acts 10:34). Only by the Holy Spirit can we see people as he sees them and feel their need as he does.

....

Lord, help us to love one another.

SEVEN

Unqualified?

IF YOU ARE AN employer looking to hire personnel for your company, you of course study the applicants very carefully. From the very first interview, you measure their abilities as best you can. You try to assess their intelligence as well as their experience for your line of work. You scrutinize their résumés; you may give certain tests. All the time you are asking yourself, *Can this person really do the job for me?*

In the book of Acts we see a number of people being chosen by the Lord for positions of great responsibility—but right away we ask, *Are these men really qualified?* They certainly did not come to their tasks with the kind of preparation we require today. A number of the apostles were only fishermen. Naturally speaking, no one would have selected them when Palestine was filled with far more promising candidates.

But through the power of the Holy Spirit, God supernaturally equipped them, surprising everyone. The question asked about them (as was asked about their Master) was, "Where did these simple men get their authority and ability?" They didn't quite "add up." Their actions were inexplicable to the natural mind.

DEACONS THEN VERSUS DEACONS NOW

When we come to Acts 6, we find more selections being made for ministry. This time it is to solve a dispute that had arisen between two ethnic groups in the church. The congregation's food program for widows—in other words, those with no way to earn their own living—was being jeopardized by complaints that one group was getting preferential treatment over the other.

I am glad this story is in the book of Acts, because it shows that everything wasn't heavenly in the early church. This congregation was growing by leaps and bounds, it was multicultural, and it had a practical ministry of caring for the needy. Still, there were irritations that came to the surface.

In response, the apostles decided to set up a seven-man team that would concentrate on this particular ministry. These became the first *deacons*, a word that comes from the Greek term for "servers." (If you thought that being a deacon means you get to sit on some prestigious board in the church, the truth is pretty much the opposite. Originally all it meant was that you rolled up your sleeves and served everyone in sight.)

Take a careful look at the qualifications for this job. The main thing the apostles put down was that deacons must be "known to be full of the Spirit and wisdom" (v. 3). It says nothing about a college degree. There is no mention of looking for people who had lots of money or business connections, which is what many churches today seem to like for their deacon boards.

A pastor friend of mine came to a very famous church in one state and told me, "I'm shocked at the deacons I've inherited here. They hardly ever show up on Sundays! There's no spiritual fiber that I can see. Apparently they were chosen because they had bucks, and to give them a board position was a way to keep them in our church instead of having them wander off somewhere else."

By contrast, the apostles knew that only if someone was full of the Spirit and wisdom would they qualify to serve effectively in the church, which is a spiritual organism requiring spiritual gifting. Degrees and business connections might be great in the corporate world, but the church's battle is "against the rulers, against the authorities, against the powers of this dark world and against the spiritual forces of evil in the heavenly realms" (Ephesians 6:12). What a tragedy when the Wall Street corporate mentality invades the church of Jesus Christ!

"FILLING" MEANS WHAT?

The apostles' job requirement that deacons be "known to be full of the Spirit" raises an interesting point. Isn't every Christian filled with the Holy Spirit? Haven't we been taught that every believer can claim this? Apparently not, or else the apostles would not have even mentioned it as a criterion.

In other words, people *not* known to be full of the Holy Spirit should not be selected. This is not to contradict Romans 8:9, which clearly teaches that "if anyone does not have the Spirit of Christ, he does not belong to Christ." The Holy Spirit is *resident* in each and every believer when one is born again into salvation. But at the same time, the New Testament shows time and again—including this passage in Acts 6—that to be *full* of the Spirit is something distinct and observable in some way. It was something that could be "known" (v. 3) about people within the Jerusalem congregation. Evidently the Holy Spirit had such control of certain people's lives that it created a reputation; they were

> Degrees and business connections might be great in the corporate world, but the church's battle is "against the rulers, against the authorities, against the powers of this dark world."

acknowledged for living victorious lives and blessing others through the Spirit's power. Only this kind of person could serve as a deacon.

The idea that all believers and all Christian churches are full of the Spirit denies both Scripture and the obvious facts around us. Why would Paul command Christians to "keep on being filled with the Spirit" (literal rendition of Ephesians 5:18) if we were filled once and for all?

The Laodicean church was clearly a Christian assembly when Jesus sent it a message (Revelation 3:14–22). But the spiritual condition of the congregation was so lukewarm that Christ was ready to vomit them out of his mouth! To maintain that they were Spirit-filled would be a gross contradiction of the evidence and would force Bible words to mean nothing. "Spirit-filled" and "lukewarm" can never go together.

And what about our churches today, where many parishioners can barely manage to show up once a week for a one-hour service (which must also be entertaining)? Can these be Spirit-filled churches? What about congregations being so concerned about black or brown people attending that they pick up and relocate whenever the neighborhood changes?

As D. L. Moody preached at the New York Hippodrome (site of the current Madison Square Garden) in 1876:

> God has got a good many children who have just barely got life, but no power for service. . . . The Holy Ghost coming upon them with power is distinct and separate from conversion. If the Scripture doesn't teach [this statement] I am ready to correct it. . . . I believe we should accomplish more in one week than we should in years if we had only this fresh baptism. . . .
>
> A great many think because they have been filled once, they are going to be full for all time after; but O, my friends, we are leaky vessels, and have to be kept

right under the fountain all the time in order to keep full. . . . Let us keep near Him.[1]

This is the problem that is least preached about, yet it is *the most critical question facing the church today.* The term *Spirit-filled* has gone into disuse in many circles since Moody's time because of certain groups who arrogantly and condescendingly *misuse* it. Often it is identified with mere emotionalism and pulpit tricks that stir the crowd. There is such a thing as Pentecostal or charismatic culture, which although often noisy is not the same as the power of Pentecost and is in fact totally predictable.

Others claim that to receive "the anointing," you must visit *their* churches, where "the River" is moving. Only by welcoming their often bizarre and unbiblical manifestations will you know that you are "in the flow."

Nowhere in the book of Acts do we see any blessing of God tied to geography. When Peter visited Cornelius in his crowded home in Caesarea, he never said, "You need to come with us back to the upper room because that's where the Holy Spirit is really moving! We had a mighty rushing wind there, and tongues of fire were over each of our heads! Jerusalem is where the fire is falling."

> **Nowhere in the book of Acts do we see any blessing of God tied to geography. . . . The early Christians didn't travel around to "get the blessing."**

The early Christians didn't travel around to "get the blessing," for they knew that the Holy Spirit is available to anyone everywhere. There is no such thing as a "Brooklyn Tabernacle anointing" or anything similar in connection with a particular church. Such claims are more egotistical than biblical. Thank God that the Holy Spirit is accessible wherever you are.

But disregarding the excesses, counterfeits, and mere cultural expressions, we must face the question, "What *does* it mean for Christians to be full of the Holy Spirit?" If we are trying to live our lives or run our churches on some other basis, we might as well throw out our Bibles. The Word of God commands us to "be *strong* in the Lord and in *his* mighty power" (Ephesians 6:10). That means it must be possible to miss the mark and be weak, not availing ourselves of the Spirit's ability.

Surprise

So these seven spiritual men were set apart, with prayer and the laying on of hands, to run the food program. Meanwhile, the apostles went back to concentrating full-time on prayer and preaching. The result, according to Acts 6:7, was explosive growth: "So the word of God spread. The number of disciples in Jerusalem increased rapidly, and a large number of [Jewish] priests became obedient to the faith."

But this story of Spirit-filled deacons is not over yet. "Now Stephen, a man full of God's grace and power, did great wonders and miraculous signs among the people" (v. 8). Stephen hadn't been ordained; he hadn't been to any seminary. He was just a faithful deacon. But out of nowhere he became a wonderful channel of ministry. Where did this come from? He wasn't an apostle; he was "just" a server.

This opened up a whole new world to the church. Until then, the early believers had assumed that God used only the twelve apostles. Now they saw that God goes beyond title. Stephen was so "full of God's grace and power" (v. 8) that he couldn't be kept in a box. If this had happened in Brooklyn, some people would have been exclaiming, "Yo! What's up with Stephen?"

Nothing in the text says Stephen was given the pulpit on Sunday morning. Nowhere does it say he joined the Twelve in their apostolic meetings. Still, the fullness of God in his life bubbled over into the marketplace, onto the street, into people's homes—you never could predict what would happen next with Deacon Stephen.

In this way God was fulfilling the promise from Joel that had been quoted back on the Day of Pentecost: "In the last days, God says, I will pour out my Spirit *on all people*. . . . Even on my servants, both men and women, I will pour out my Spirit in those days" (Acts 2:17–18). Not just people called "Reverend." Not just official pastors. Not just staff personnel. This experience was for anyone and everyone among God's people.

> The issue for God is not ability but availability. There is no such thing as "only an usher" or "only a nursery worker."

No one could have anticipated this. It went against all precedent and tradition. But boom! There was Stephen, out making waves for the kingdom of God.

The church today needs to stop and understand anew that God does not work by titles or human resources but by divine gifting. As we noted in chapter 3, the issue for God is not ability but availability. There is no such thing as "only an usher" or "only a nursery worker." The Bible says that "with God all things are possible" (Matthew 19:26), including supernatural things as we recover faith in the power of the Holy Spirit.

ON TRACK—AND IN MAJOR TROUBLE

Soon enough, opposition rose up—not from the church members, thank God, but from unbelievers. (Would that we could say as much today when God uses someone unusual in our churches. At least Stephen's fellow believers seem to have supported and encouraged him rather than criticizing his lack of qualifications.)

Jewish antagonists began to argue with Stephen. They misrepresented his views and trumped up phony accusations. The situation got nasty. They found that "they could not stand up against his wisdom or the Spirit by whom he spoke" (Acts 6:10). Stephen was getting divine assistance right on the spot. No wonder his opponents brought out the handcuffs and dragged him off!

Have you ever heard a modern preacher declare that if you're right with God and just repeat the promises, everything will work out fine and dandy? You just take authority over any problem or circumstance, and it will all melt away like the snow.

Well, I have to tell you that Stephen, "a man *full of faith* and of the Holy Spirit" (v. 5), got busted. "They seized Stephen and brought him before the Sanhedrin" (v. 12). Then it got worse as charges were hurled at him. People lied about him and slandered him. Most of Acts 7 is a court transcript of how the trial went.

> We can be in the very center of God's will, being used by the Lord in a powerful way—and still get into a lot of trouble. The Bible doesn't have Hollywood endings to every story.

Was Stephen delivered in the end? No. He became the first martyr of the Christian faith. He died a horrible death by stoning, yet he spoke boldly for Christ to the very end. This goes to show us that we can be in the very center of God's will, being used by the Lord in a powerful way—and still get into a lot of trouble. The Bible doesn't have Hollywood endings to every story. It clearly shows us that being God's child involves more than just spiritual euphoria all day long.

Romans 8:17 says, "If we are children, then we are heirs—heirs of God and co-heirs with Christ, *if indeed we share in his sufferings* in order that we may also share in his glory." Remember that the main question is not *if* we will die someday, but rather *how* we will die. We must remain fervent for Christ to the very end as Stephen did.

One member of the vicious mob that day was a fellow off to the side named Saul, from the city of Tarsus up north in Asia Minor. We don't know what he was thinking, other than that he was "giving approval to his [Stephen's] death" (Acts 8:1). His rage against the Christians continued for a while longer . . . but the day came, on the Damascus road, when Christ spoke from heaven, "Saul, Saul, why do you persecute me?" (Acts 9:4). Saul fell to the ground in repentance, and that is how we came to receive the priceless ministry of this great apostle.

UNFORESEEN FRUIT

It may well be that something was sown in the heart of Saul that day as he watched Stephen die, something that bore fruit later on. As a result, scores of churches were planted across the Roman Empire, thousands of people came to salvation in Christ, and half the New Testament flowed from his pen to benefit us all to this very day.

Back in 1921, a missionary couple named David and Svea Flood went with their two-year-old son from Sweden to the heart of Africa—to what was then called the Belgian Congo. They met up with another young Scandinavian couple, the Ericksons, and the four of them sought God for direction. In those days of much tenderness and devotion and sacrifice, they felt led of the Lord to set out from the main mission station and take the gospel to a remote area.

This was a huge step of faith. At the village of N'dolera they were rebuffed by the chief, who would not let them enter his town for fear of alienating the local gods. The two couples opted to go half a mile up the slope and build their own mud huts.

They prayed for a spiritual breakthrough, but there was none. The only contact with the villagers was a young boy, who was allowed to sell them chickens and eggs twice a week. Svea Flood—a tiny woman only four feet, eight inches tall—decided that if this was the only African she could talk to, she would try to lead the boy to Jesus. And in fact, she succeeded.

But there were no other encouragements. Meanwhile, malaria continued to strike one member of the little band after another. In time the Ericksons decided they had had enough suffering and left to return to the central mission station. David and Svea Flood remained near N'dolera to go on alone.

Then, of all things, Svea found herself pregnant in the middle of the primitive wilderness. When the time came for her to give birth, the village chief softened enough to allow a midwife to help her. A little girl was born, whom they named Aina.

The delivery, however, was exhausting, and Svea Flood was already weak from bouts of malaria. The birth process was a heavy blow to her stamina. She lasted only another seventeen days.

Inside David Flood, something snapped in that moment. He dug a crude grave, buried his twenty-seven-year-old wife, and then took his children back down the mountain to the mission station. Giving his newborn daughter to the Ericksons, he snarled, "I'm going back to Sweden. I've lost my wife, and I obviously can't take care of this baby. God has ruined my life." With that, he headed for the port, rejecting not only his calling, but God himself.

Within eight months both the Ericksons were stricken with a mysterious malady and died within days of each other. The baby was then turned over to some American missionaries, who adjusted her Swedish name to "Aggie" and eventually brought her back to the United States at age three.

This family loved the little girl and were afraid that if they tried to return to Africa, some legal obstacle might separate her from them. So they decided to stay in their home country and switch from missionary work to pastoral ministry. And that is how Aggie grew up in South Dakota. As a young woman, she attended North Central Bible College in Minneapolis. There she met and married a young man named Dewey Hurst.

Years passed. The Hursts enjoyed a fruitful ministry. Aggie gave birth first to a daughter, then a son. In time her husband became president of a Christian college in the Seattle area, and Aggie was intrigued to find so much Scandinavian heritage there.

One day a Swedish religious magazine appeared in her mailbox. She had no idea who had sent it, and of course she couldn't read the words. But as she turned the pages, all of a sudden a photo stopped her cold. There in a primitive setting was a grave with a white cross—and on the cross were the words SVEA FLOOD.

Aggie jumped in her car and went straight for a college faculty member who, she knew, could translate the article. "What does this say?" she demanded.

The instructor summarized the story: It was about missionaries who had come to N'dolera long ago ... the birth of a white baby ... the death of the young mother ... the one little African boy who had been led to Christ ... and how, after the whites had all left, the boy had grown up and finally persuaded the chief to let him build a school in the village.

The article said that gradually he won all his students to Christ ... the children led their parents to Christ ... even the chief had become a Christian. Today there were six hundred Christian believers in that one village. ...

All because of the sacrifice of David and Svea Flood.

For the Hursts' twenty-fifth wedding anniversary, the college presented them with the gift of a vacation to Sweden. There Aggie sought to find her real father. An old man now, David Flood had remarried, fathered four more children, and generally dissipated his life with alcohol. He had recently suffered a stroke. Still bitter, he had one rule in his family: "Never mention the name of God—because God took everything from me."

After an emotional reunion with her half brothers and half sister, Aggie brought up the subject of seeing her father. The others hesitated. "You can talk to him," they replied, "even though he's very ill now. But you need to know that whenever he hears the name of God, he flies into a rage."

Aggie was not to be deterred. She walked into the squalid apartment, with liquor bottles everywhere, and approached the seventy-three-year-old man lying in a rumpled bed.

"Papa?" she said tentatively.

He turned and began to cry. "Aina," he said. "I never meant to give you away."

"It's all right, Papa," she replied, taking him gently in her arms. "God took care of me."

The man instantly stiffened. The tears stopped.

"God forgot all of us. Our lives have been like this because of him." He turned his face back to the wall.

Aggie stroked his face and then continued, undaunted.

"Papa, I've got a little story to tell you, and it's a true one. You didn't go to Africa in vain. Mama didn't die in vain. The little boy you won to the Lord grew up to win that whole village to Jesus Christ. The one seed you planted just kept growing and growing. Today there are six hundred African people serving the Lord because you were faithful to the call of God in your life. . . .

"Papa, Jesus loves you. He has never hated you."

The old man turned back to look into his daughter's eyes. His body relaxed. He began to talk. And by the end of the afternoon, he had come back to the God he had resented for so many decades.

Over the next few days, father and daughter enjoyed warm moments together. Aggie and her husband soon had to return to America—and within a few weeks, David Flood had gone into eternity.

A few years later, the Hursts were attending a high-level evangelism conference in London, England, when a report was given from the nation of Zaire (the former Belgian Congo). The superintendent of the national church, representing some 110,000 baptized believers, spoke eloquently of the gospel's spread in his nation. Aggie could not help going to ask him afterward if he had ever heard of David and Svea Flood.

"Yes, madam," the man replied in French, his words then being translated into English. "It was Svea Flood who led me to Jesus Christ. I was the boy who brought food to your parents before you were born. In fact, to this day your mother's grave and her memory are honored by all of us."

He embraced her in a long, sobbing hug. Then he continued, "You must come to Africa to see, because your mother is the most famous person in our history."

In time that is exactly what Aggie Hurst and her husband did. They were welcomed by cheering throngs of villagers. She even met the man who had been hired by her father many years before to carry her back down the mountain in a hammock-cradle.

The most dramatic moment, of course, was when the pastor escorted Aggie to see her mother's white cross for herself. She knelt in the soil to pray and give thanks. Later that day, in the church, the pastor read from John 12:24: "I tell you the truth, unless a kernel of wheat falls to the ground and dies, it remains only a single seed. But if it dies, it produces many seeds." He then followed with Psalm 126:5: "Those who sow in tears will reap with songs of joy."[2]

A STANDING OVATION

The sacrifice of Svea Flood is a fitting parallel to the sacrifice of the early deacon Stephen. They both gave their all, not counting the cost and not expecting to be rescued before pain and suffering would strike. They both died far too young by human standards. And yet their accomplishments in the spiritual realm are beyond measuring.

At the last minute Stephen received a vision to encourage him. Acts 7:56 says he saw "heaven open and the Son of Man *standing* at the right hand of God." Throughout the epistles and the book of Revelation, Jesus is usually described as *sitting* on his throne alongside the Father. But it seems this was such a climactic moment that Jesus *stood up*. Stephen was coming home.

How we live is more important than *how long* we live. What is the sense of living a long life just to hang around and take up space? I would rather live a few meaningful, fruitful years for Christ than hang on to age eighty-nine and accomplish little.

Even with all the advancements of modern medicine helping us live longer, our lives are still a momentary vapor compared with eternity. Not one material thing we possess will go with us as we leave this world. The physical world that so easily grabs our attention and affections will have absolutely no meaning to us one split second after we cross over.

I want to be totally yielded to God, don't you? I don't want to live half full; I want to experience what it means to be *full* of the Holy Spirit in the way God intended. He promised that through the gospel and the Spirit's anointing, our lives could be used just like Svea Flood's to bring blessing and hope to multitudes. The thought of that means far more to me than any worldly honor or achievement. I don't want a title; I don't want to be famous or meet some earthly dignitary; I don't want to be rich. I just want God to clothe me with his Spirit so I can affect people for Christ.

May God help us to live for something far greater than ourselves, far greater than "the cravings of sinful man, the lust of his eyes and the boasting of what he has and does," for these things do not come "from the Father but from the world. The world and its desires pass away, but the man who does the will of God lives forever" (1 John 2:16–17).

We have the opportunity right now to draw near to God in prayer, knowing that he will be faithful to draw near to us. Only the Lord can deliver us from busy, cluttered living that so easily drifts from the plan God has for our lives, from the spiritual fruit we can produce for his glory. What stops us at this moment from asking God to melt our hearts and soften our wills so we can be doers, not just hearers, of his Word?

....

Dear Father, forgive us for often ignoring your purpose for our lives. Pardon us for the sin of small and selfish living, with little thought of the privilege and potential in belonging to you. Reveal your will and purpose concerning us, and then give us the grace to pursue it with all of our hearts. We ask this in Christ's name. Amen.

EIGHT

Getting People Out of
Their Prisons

I BELIEVE THAT NEARLY all church leaders and mature believers across our country today would agree that we urgently need spiritual revival. In some exceptional places the Lord is obviously blessing, but in the vast majority of our churches, no matter the denomination, we are not seeing the kind of evangelistic growth and spiritual vitality modeled in the book of Acts.

The plain truth is that we are not baptizing large numbers of people in proportion to the population. Researchers have now proven that most of the much-heralded "church growth" is little more than people moving from First Presbyterian to First Nazarene to First Baptist to First Assembly of God. That is not what causes the angels to rejoice. They rejoice when a *sinner* repents.

Part of our problem is that we have developed a religious industry whose machinery runs smoothly without any need of the Holy Spirit. A. W. Tozer once commented that if God were to take the Holy Spirit out of this world, most of what the church is doing would go right on, and nobody would know the difference. We have become set in our ways—but they are not the ways of God's blessing and power.

The churches in Acts had no New Testament (it wasn't written yet), no choirs, no electronic gear, no buildings of their own, no friends in high places—and yet they still shook the world. God didn't send the Holy Spirit to give us thrills and chills; he sent the Spirit to empower us to win lost people to Jesus. The acid test of my preaching and our choir's ministry is whether, through God, we are able to pierce hard, unbelieving hearts with the gospel message and see people turn to the Lord. Without this divine power and boldness we tend to shy away from confronting the world head-on. We retreat into discussions about how terrible everything is around us. Or else we argue endlessly with each other about whose doctrine is more correct. Church becomes a cultural club for sociologists to study.

> **God didn't send the Holy Spirit to give us thrills and chills; he sent the Spirit to empower us to win lost people to Jesus.**

We need to pray for revival of such power that we resemble more of the early church in the book of Acts. In that golden age there was liberty and freedom under God—you never quite knew what was going to happen. The Holy Spirit could manifest himself at any moment. Yet there was careful Bible teaching as well. This balance between the Word and the Spirit is a great challenge today, when the pendulum swings between fanaticism and dry orthodoxy are so strong.

Many current church leaders think the goal is to rigidly control every phase of God's work. I humbly disagree. We are probably organized far too much. The early church had a beautiful spontaneity and freshness, without being chaotic or disorderly.

D. L. Moody once said,

> The Spirit of God ... first imparts love; He next inspires hope; and then He gives liberty—which is

about the last thing we have in a good many of our churches at the present day. I am sorry to say there must be a funeral in a good many churches before there is much work done; we shall have to bury the formalism so deep that it will never have any resurrection. The last thing to be found in many a church is liberty.[1]

What often holds us back is what I call "cultural religion"—our blind devotion to the way we were raised in church and the atmosphere we experienced every Sunday. I thank God for every good thing learned in the past, every blessing received—but doesn't the Lord have more for us? Are we making such an impact on the world for God that we can't humble ourselves in prayer for a change in the status quo? Revival comes when people get dissatisfied with *what is* and yearn deeply for *what could be*.

> "I am sorry to say there must be a funeral in a good many churches before there is much work done; we shall have to bury the formalism."
> —D. L. Moody

One of the distinguishing traits of the early church was their practice of serious prayer. The apostles had never said, "Lord, teach us to preach" or "Lord, teach us to lead worship." But they *had* asked, "Lord, teach us to pray" (Luke 11:1). Something about Jesus' ability to commune with his Father in heaven fascinated them.

When the Holy Spirit was poured out upon them, he birthed a new spirit of prayer and intercession. They began following a simple practice: The best thing to do whenever emergencies come is to gather to pray! It was a living reality to them that God responds when people call upon his name. Indeed, this faith and fervency was begotten by the Spirit of God.

This is one of the spiritual facts of life that hungry pastors are coming to grasp more and more. They have been stirred by God to want a real change in their churches, especially in the matter of corporate prayer. But their zeal to initiate prayer meetings (of one kind or another) often turns to gloom as they see their members uninterested and unmoved. Even those who attend the prayer services are often cold and mechanical, with little or no sense of that effectual, fervent praying mentioned in Scripture.

The root problem is the need for the Holy Spirit to come in power and birth a true spirit of prayer. In other words, we must first secure the Spirit's presence and grace; then we can move out in powerful praying for all kinds of other needs. Let us remember the Lord's promise: "If you then, though you are evil, know how to give good gifts to your children, how much more will your Father in heaven give the Holy Spirit to those who ask him!" (Luke 11:13).

THE COUNTDOWN

One of the first crises for the early church began with the martyrdom of the apostle James, recorded in the opening verses of Acts 12. And hardly before they could get James buried, Peter was arrested. The believers must have gasped and said to one another, "What's going on? Herod is going to pick off our leaders one after another!"

The king would have quickly executed Peter except that the calendar got in his way. Just then it happened to be Passover Week, so Herod had to wait until the next normal business day. (He was apparently fussy about having innocent people killed on Jewish holy days.)

What was the church going to do? They could have given in to what seemed inevitable. But no, the Bible reports, "So Peter was kept in prison, *but the church was earnestly praying to God for him*" (Acts 12:5). They wrestled in prayer; a continual stream of intercession went up to heaven for Peter, who needed a miraculous deliverance.

I suppose they could have organized a political demonstration demanding respect for Peter's civil rights, protesting the obvious discrimination against Christians. Instead, they clung to the Lord's promises: "Ask and it will be given to you; seek and you will find; knock and the door will be opened to you. For everyone who asks receives; he who seeks finds; and to him who knocks, the door will be opened" (Matthew 7:7–8).

Every evening, as the Passover Week dragged on, you could see clusters of Christians scurrying through the shadows toward homes all over Jerusalem. There they would stay until the early hours of the morning, crying out, "Oh, God, spare Peter's life! We've already lost James, and we'll lose Peter, too, unless you intervene. Our eyes are on you. No one else can help but you."

They couldn't physically get to Peter; they could not go to his cell to encourage him, lay hands on him, or anything else. But what is unreachable physically is still accessible spiritually. Prayer moves the hand of God, a hand that is omnipotent.

Think of the blessings and miraculous answers we are missing today by not taking God at his word. He has never changed—but we have moved a long way in our thinking from those earnest seekers of two thousand years ago.

Isn't it obvious that if preaching alone were the answer, we would have seen a different America long ago? If good gospel music, radio programs, and plush sanctuaries were the key, we would

> **If preaching alone were the answer, we would have seen a different America long ago. If good gospel music, radio programs, and plush sanctuaries were the key, we would know it by now.**

know it by now. Prayer is the avenue God uses to come and bless his people.

Every first week of January we shut down the normal schedule at the Brooklyn Tabernacle for a series of nightly prayer meetings. No other activities or programs go on that week because we know all too well that we must be strong in the Lord for whatever challenges or satanic attacks the new year might hold. The building is filled to overflowing each night with people seeking the Lord and waiting in his presence.

The next week we return to our regular rhythm of ongoing Tuesday night prayer meetings plus the other classes and activities. Our Prayer Band, headed by Associate Pastor Ken Ware, has a rotating contingent in our building interceding at the throne of grace twenty-four hours a day, seven days a week, with no interruption. At certain times during the year we have also opened up the church in the late afternoons for corporate prayer after work.

Having said all this, I must still admit that our church needs a fresh visitation of God's Spirit, and all our leadership knows it. Yes, we thank God for his blessings, the evidence of his grace all around us. But there is so much more to receive from him. We are just scratching the surface of what we know God can and will do in and through us.

THE DELIVERANCE

The Passover Week winds down. The sun sets on the Sabbath. The believers grow more earnest than ever as they gather again. "Oh, God, we're running out of time! The holiday is over now. This is the last night; tomorrow could be the end. The final hours are upon us, O Lord. Save Peter, we pray!"

And just in time . . . God sends his angel to the dark cell.

The night before Herod was to bring him to trial, Peter was sleeping between two soldiers, bound with two chains, and sentries stood guard at the entrance. Suddenly an angel of the Lord appeared and a light shone in the cell. He struck Peter on the side and woke him up. "Quick, get up!" he said, and the chains fell off Peter's wrists (Acts 12:6–7).

Isn't that like God to send his answer *just in time!* At the very last moment, Peter was rescued; the church's prayers were answered. That is the way it will be for you and me if we just keep holding on in faith. God's clock is not like ours. Over and over in Scripture, he comes on the scene just in time.

Once again in this narrative, we see God sending "something from heaven." In this case, an angel came to rescue God's servant. The angel appeared along with a "bright light" that cut through the dank darkness of Peter's cell. What a wonderful picture of the divine illumination God can send to dispel our confusion and bewilderment.

How many of us today are facing pitch-dark dilemmas in our marriages, among our children, or in our finances? Possibly a spiritual problem is nagging at us, with seemingly no solution. We have reasoned and counseled and strategized, all to no avail. What we need is a burst of God's light.

It is the same kind of light we need every time we open the Bible. "The man without the Spirit does not accept the things that come from the Spirit of God" (1 Corinthians 2:14), and this certainly includes our need of revelation from God, a definite teaching to our heart of what Scripture really means. The Hebrew or Greek scholar will never by natural processes fully understand the depths hidden in God's Word. *Lord, send us more light!*

The angel struck Peter that night to wake him up, for he was not praying for himself; he was sleeping. Many of us have loved ones and friends who are in another kind of sleep—a spiritual stupor, which is far more deadly. Some of them may have served the Lord in the past.

Just as God woke up Peter in answer to his people's earnest praying, we can trust God to come and do it again. He can awaken them to the spiritual realities of heaven, hell, and salvation. I have seen many, many of these answers to prayer in our congregation. We need to be praying as never before: *Wake them up, Lord! Wake them up.*

Even after having been awakened, Peter still had two soldiers nearby, sentries at the gate, and chains binding him. God somehow dispensed with the guards, and the chains fell off Peter's wrists as the angel spoke to him. I want to declare unequivocally that God still breaks chains today—no matter how strong the shackles of lust, drugs, alcohol, or deceit. The Spirit's power can break these fetters and set men and women free.

FREE ON THE INSIDE

Perhaps the most dramatic deliverance of our time is what God has done for a nationally known, nationally feared criminal called "Son of Sam" or "The .44-Caliber Killer." To set the stage for this spiritual rescue, I take you back to the summer of 1977. We had recently moved our Sunday services from the tiny building on Atlantic Avenue in downtown Brooklyn to a nearby YWCA, which had an auditorium that seated about five hundred. Carol and I were happy for the extra space, but with no air conditioning in the building and with all the windows painted shut, the months of July and August offered special challenges. I still remember one outreach service when the temperature must have reached 110 degrees in the densely packed room.

Things were blazing in New York City that summer, and I am referring to more than the weather. It was open season for a crazed gunman who shot young women and then wrote sick letters to the newspapers about his homicidal spree. He said he was getting his orders to kill from a dog, and the entire city was terrified.

The word on the street was that he targeted brunettes. All kinds of women bleached their hair to avoid becoming his next victim. New York City is probably the most sophisticated metropolis in the world, but one anonymous man had brought it under a palpable cloud of terror. It was *the* topic of conversation every day and everywhere, from affluent Upper East Side tearooms to the alleys of Skid Row. Newspaper headlines each day brought new information—or guesses—about how the killer operated. The pressure on the New York Police Department to apprehend him was tremendous.

Suddenly the killer struck again, and another family mourned the loss of their daughter. Again, not a trace of evidence was left for the authorities. Again, the vice of fear tightened around a seemingly helpless city. What kind of fiend was this, we wondered, randomly shooting young women for no apparent reason?

> The vice of fear tightened around a seemingly helpless city. What kind of fiend was this, we wondered, randomly shooting young women for no apparent reason?

After thirteen months the case finally broke. David Berkowitz, a twenty-four-year-old postal worker living in Yonkers, a suburb just north of the city, was arrested. A parking ticket issued near the site of his last shooting led the police to him at last. For days all you could see on television was "Son of Sam," handcuffed and surrounded by officers. His eyes had a spaced-out look, but there was also a strange smirk on his face. We all slept better those nights in the Big Apple.

When taken to court, David Berkowitz openly pleaded guilty to killing five women and one man as well as wounding many others. Only New York State's ban on the death penalty kept him alive. His prison sentence ran to hundreds of years as he was shipped off to Attica.

I gradually forgot about him . . . until a few years ago when a woman I didn't know called the church office and asked to speak to me. After introducing herself, she said, "Do you remember the name David Berkowitz—the serial killer from the late seventies?"

"Of course," I replied. "I was living right here in New York during all that."

"Well, David has become a believer," she said. Carol and I had seen a brief news story about his putting his faith in Christ, but we had no details.

"A Christian group is trying to publicize his testimony, and he's uncomfortable with the way they're going about it. But he knows of you by watching your choir videos there in prison, and he trusts you. Do you think you could help him?"

"Have him call me," I replied.

And that is exactly what happened. In the subsequent months I developed a telephone friendship with a man I never dreamed of meeting under any circumstances, much less as a fellow Christian. We talked several times on the phone and exchanged letters. Gradually I heard about his early life, how he had grown up in the Bronx as an adopted child in a Jewish home.

"I was troubled psychologically and emotionally from early on," David told me, "and I proved to be a real handful for my parents. I felt somehow drawn to evil and occultic things—was fascinated by it, in fact. It seemed that even as a child I was marked and cultivated by Satan for evil purposes."

School was nothing but one problem after another. David's disruptive behavior had all the officials trying to bring him under control. At home he would crawl under his bed for hours at a time. Late at night he would use the fire escape to leave his bedroom and roam the dark streets. Horror movies were his favorite.

David's adoptive mother was a practicing Jew who kept a kosher house and celebrated Jewish holy days. Gentile kids in the neighborhood occasionally taunted David with anti-Semitic remarks, but he didn't really identify with any religion. The person and name of Jesus Christ meant nothing specific to him. "I honestly thought he was just some kind of Catholic guy! I had no idea Jesus claimed to be the Messiah of Israel."

Somehow David finished high school and joined the army. Three years later, he returned to the Bronx to find old friends. But most of the guys he used to know were gone now, and some had not survived the mean streets of the city. "I was lonely, just looking for someone to hang out with. I got a job, rented an apartment, and furnished it with the hope of maybe meeting a nice girl. I just wanted to live some kind of normal life. But that was not to be."

David was vulnerable, and his emptiness of soul began drawing him to people and things that were increasingly dark. The satanic group he joined was bent on creating mayhem. Armageddon was soon to happen anyway, they figured, so why not start the chaos right now? David began hauling big rocks onto overpasses and tossing them into the traffic below just to watch the accidents that would result. He then escalated into setting fires of all kinds—2,000 of them altogether, which he carefully logged in a journal.

"I started praying and talking to demons," he sadly recalled. "Gradually I became very delusional. I was convinced that demons were talking to me and trying to guide me through barking dogs. I was losing my mind."

In time David began picking off young women on dimly lit streets and in lovers' lanes with their boyfriends, using a .44-caliber handgun. "Nothing could control me. I was like the tormented Gadarene demoniac—anguished, inflicting pain on myself, and driven into dark and lonely places."

With his arrest and conviction, David's reputation preceded him to prison, of course. In 1979 he almost died when a razor-wielding inmate slashed him, apparently trying to make a name for himself. The attack opened up the left side of David's neck like the flap of an envelope. The medical personnel who stitched him up couldn't understand how his carotid artery had not been severed. A major scar remains today.

In 1987 David was moved to Sullivan Correctional Facility, about two hours' drive northwest of my home. One cold December night while walking in the exercise yard, he was approached by a young prisoner named Ricky Lopez. "He said he wanted to tell me something—that Jesus loved me and had a purpose for my life. I laughed him off and said he didn't know who he was talking to. I added that no one could love someone who had committed such horrible crimes.

"He said he knew exactly who I was, but it didn't matter. Jesus still loved me and wanted to have a personal relationship with me."

Ricky kept walking alongside David day after day, becoming his friend. Then one day he presented him with a small New Testament with Psalms and suggested that, since David was Jewish, he might start reading the Psalms.

Back in his cell, David began to read. Psalm 18 especially struck him:

I call to the LORD, who is worthy of praise,
    and I am saved from my enemies. . . .
In my distress I called to the LORD;
    I cried to my God for help.
From his temple he heard my voice;
    my cry came before him, into his ears (vv. 3, 6).

Another poignant verse was Psalm 34:6: "This poor man called, and the LORD heard him; he saved him out of all his troubles."

The Word of God penetrated David's heart. He soon knelt by his bunk and asked Jesus Christ to be his Savior and Lord. He wept as he laid aside the tremendous condemnation he felt for what he had done, which was bearing down upon him all the more clearly now. The Word was working in him, and he cried out for mercy.

Over the past decade and more, David Berkowitz has progressed in his faith. He is a diligent student of God's Word. He is now the chaplain's assistant at Sullivan. He has coordinated more than one concert by the choir from Manhattan Grace Tabernacle, one of our daughter churches. On their first visit, as they were setting up equipment and adjusting the sound system, David happened to walk in from the back and quietly asked if he could help them or get anything they needed. Several choir members who had lived through his reign of terror began to weep at the sight of him and the obvious change in his personality.

Eventually Carol and I went to see him ourselves. We found him to be one of the kindest, gentlest Christians we have ever had the pleasure of meeting. Carol asked him, "David, how can we help you? Can we bring you anything from the outside that you need?"

All that this humble, now middle-aged man could answer was "Just pray for me. I sometimes get lonely. The cellblock is so noisy sometimes that it's hard for me to read the Word or to pray. But I know that I need the Holy Spirit to keep me strong in the Lord."

We told him how our church's drama team had put together a presentation of his life to communicate the gospel, and it had twice packed our building. He just dropped his head and softly said, "Thank you, Jesus. All praise to you, Jesus."

David has now spent half his life behind bars. He will never be paroled. In fact, he has never asked me or any other minister or organization to plead for his release. He knows his crimes were so serious that he deserves to be locked up for life, and he says the prison is his God-ordained sphere of ministry. Sometimes the chaplain or the inmate worship leader will allow David to lead a Bible study or a service, even to preach at times when a scheduled civilian minister is unable to come. To leave this setting, he says, would be to run from the call of God on his life, the way Jonah did. "There's plenty to do here," David says.

"But it's dangerous as well. God has warned me many times when something was about to 'go down.'"

David has become a dear friend to Carol and me. Not only that, but he is my brother in Christ, for God has changed the very "chief of sinners"—a demon-controlled serial killer—into a precious child of God. The strongest satanic chains have been broken by the Lord Jesus Christ.

In the two thousand years since Christ's death and resurrection, has there ever been such a miracle of deliverance? God broke those fetters for "Son of Sam." He is free in his spirit to follow the Savior he loves. In the corridors of heaven you and I will be mingling with him, our brother in Christ.

What chains have formed in your own life? What son or daughter is too far away from God? In what prison of depression or guilt are you locked? "If the Son sets you free, you will be free indeed" (John 8:36).

DOORS MUST OPEN

When God moves into our lives, no obstacle can stop him. In the book of Acts, the rest of Peter's story illustrates this wonderful truth.

> Then the angel said to him, "Put on your clothes and sandals." And Peter did so. "Wrap your cloak around you and follow me," the angel told him. Peter followed him out of the prison, but he had no idea that what the angel was doing was really happening; he thought he was seeing a vision. They passed the first and second guards and came to the iron gate leading to the city. It opened for them by itself, and they went through it. When they had walked the length of one street, suddenly the angel left him.
>
> Then Peter came to himself and said, "Now I know without a doubt that the Lord sent his angel and rescued me from Herod's clutches and from everything the Jewish people were anticipating" (Acts 12:8–11).

Notice that the angel and Peter had to confront the iron gate that led to the city. This was the final obstacle. On the other side lay freedom. The Bible says, *"It opened for them by itself,* and they went through it" (v. 10). No fumbling with a key, no battering ram. The last obstacle blocking Peter's freedom surrendered before the power of the Lord.

This is such a word of encouragement to me whenever I read this passage. Aren't you and I tired of struggling to open doors within our own strength? It might be a door of opportunity for greater service to God, or a door of resistance that bars us from stepping out to a new place in God. There are so many kinds of doors we confront when we serve Jesus and wrestle against the powers of darkness.

But God can do more in one day than we can accomplish in ten years of human effort. I have spent months laboring to push doors open that only God could release, and I am still learning that far more is accomplished by persevering in prayer than in taking charge of things myself.

I am so glad I heard as a child this simple little prayer chorus, which still blesses me every time I sing it:

> *Jesus breaks every fetter*
> *Jesus breaks every fetter*
> *Jesus breaks every fetter*
> *And he sets me free.*

NINE

Holy Spirit "Strategy"

WHEN I WAS ONLY ten years old, my brother, Bob, gave me a paperback book on how to play basketball. Written by Red Auerbach, the legendary coach, general manager, and owner of the Boston Celtics, it was an excellent treatment of the fundamentals: footwork, defense, shooting, how to dribble the ball, how to pass, how to box out, how to fake. Soon I was trying out what I had learned in a little church gymnasium. Every Saturday morning Bob and I would get on the city bus, change to a second bus, and finally arrive at Quincy Street in the Bedford-Stuyvesant area of Brooklyn, where for up to three hours we would shoot baskets until my little arms were drooping.

Then it was back home to the bedroom we shared, where I would pull out the book once again to study the instructions, imagine the moves, and linger over the pictures of the great Celtic players such as Bob Cousy and Tommy Heinsohn. In my boyhood eagerness I would practice in front of a mirror: *Fake left, go right*, just as Red Auerbach said.

The book was good . . . but as I grew older and started playing on my high school team, I found out what every athlete knows: Although it's important to learn the fundamentals, they will never by themselves make you a champion. When you get into a game, you have to go with an inner sense of what will work instant by instant. I have seen players who have all the basics down pat but are still stiff and mechanical. They don't seem to have that special sense that expresses itself in a smooth flow. That is why they will never get near the rhythm of a Magic Johnson, a Larry Bird, or a Michael Jordan.

I remember watching game films during my college days at the University of Rhode Island and seeing myself do things on the floor that I didn't remember at all. In fact, I had never consciously thought about doing them. I just reacted as the game unfolded before me. Suddenly I was spinning to the left for no reason other than that my instincts told me to do so.

God intended his work—everything from teaching a Sunday school class to pioneering a brand-new missionary effort—to be marked by a similar flow of a spiritual kind. The Bible calls it being "led by the Spirit" (Romans 8:14; Galatians 5:18). Yes, there are important doctrinal principles to learn and biblical facts to nail down, but at the same time, only God the Holy Spirit can weave them all together in a seamless, almost unconscious way so we can touch people with God's message of love. What we need is that unique merger of divine truth, human personality, and Holy Spirit gifting that produces effective ministry for Christ.

PLAYERS AND "WATCHERS"

The living Spirit of God can give us direction at critical moments. He can indicate to us what to say, what not to say, and how to react to the onrush of satanic schemes. He gives us the mind of Christ and spiritual clarity regarding what we are really up against. He imparts wisdom and discernment that no school can teach. These are absolute essentials if we are to be "competent as ministers of a new covenant—not of the letter but of the Spirit; for the letter kills, but the Spirit gives life"

(2 Corinthians 3:6). Equipped by God, we can successfully compete in the great spiritual contest called gospel work.

But just as there are people who watch from the bleachers and never know the challenge of competing on the court, we have millions of churchgoers who sit in pews every week without ever entering the game. They sacrifice nothing, strain toward no ministry goals, never agonize in prayer for one soul, but pass judgment on how well the contest of faith is being played. Often they act as if "they know." It looks easy from where they're sitting, but then again, they have never really attempted much for God.

The Christian who is willing to risk body and soul in the struggle against evil is of a different mind. He knows there will be difficult moments and all kinds of pressure. He knows he will need to summon all his strength as well as God's in order to prevail. He is a champion for God, and he dares to plunge into the contest.

We read about two such valiant warriors in Acts 13 and how they started a historic ministry for Christ. It all began with the leaders of the Antioch church—a clearly multiracial group, by the way— doing something very strange, at least to our modern ears. "While they were worshiping the Lord and fasting, the Holy Spirit said, 'Set apart for me Barnabas and Saul for the work to which I have called them.' So after they had fasted and prayed, they placed their hands on them and sent them off" (vv. 2–3). And so Paul's First Missionary Journey, as it is called, was launched, affecting the whole future of the Christian religion.

> **"Most people plot and plan themselves into mediocrity, while now and again somebody forgets himself into greatness."**
> **—E. Stanley Jones**

These men were not sitting in a boardroom making strategic charts on a whiteboard. They were not huddled around their computers working on spreadsheets. Instead, they were having a time of worship, praise, and prayer, all intensified by periods of fasting. E. Stanley Jones said in one of his early books, "Most people plot and plan themselves into mediocrity, while now and again somebody forgets himself into greatness."[1] The brothers in Antioch forgot about legitimate things such as food in order to heighten their awareness of the spiritual realm. God the Holy Spirit seems drawn to such times. When we wait on him in this way, he speaks to us and tells us what we need to hear.

But if we are always busy working, doing, talking, handing out materials, and fielding phone calls, we miss the chances to listen and get our ears tuned to his voice. These men in Antioch quieted down enough to hear something from heaven.

Samuel Chadwick said in the early 1900s, "The church that multiplies committees and neglects prayer may be fussy, noisy, enterprising, but it labors in vain and spends its strength for naught. It is possible to excel in mechanics and fail in dynamics. There is an abundance of machinery; what is wanting is power."[2]

The Holy Spirit Wants *You*

In the Old Testament we often read that "God said such-and-such." Likewise, in the gospels there are dozens of places where "Jesus said. ..." Now the same pattern appears in the book of Acts, only in this case, "the Holy Spirit said. ..." This, too, is a living, speaking, divine person, the third member of the Trinity. He gives divine leading on what to do in order to advance the church.

All of us who say we want to build the kingdom of God must stop and admit our need of divine leading. There must be a living interaction between us and the Holy Spirit or else we will not get far. He must show us how to carry out the Great Commission of the church effectively, both in evangelism and in discipleship.

We don't know precisely how the Holy Spirit expressed himself that day in Antioch, but it seems reasonable to assume that it was some kind of spiritual gift, perhaps what 1 Corinthians 12 calls "prophecy." The directive of the Spirit came through human instruments.

What he said was, "Set apart *for me* Barnabas and Saul." The Spirit was claiming these two men for a special mission. Think of the spiritual drama as the living Spirit put his finger on these two individuals in the midst of the other leaders and possibly the whole congregation.

The Spirit has his own strategy and plans for the church. Notice the wording of verse 2: "... for the work to which *I* have called them." Who could ever possibly direct the affairs of the Christian church better than the Holy Spirit? If he gave specific instructions for the work back then, what verse in the Bible says he doesn't do it now? What has changed about us or the world that we don't need his specific leadings on who, what, when, and where?

Missionary organizations and church board meetings that do not include times of prayer and waiting on God for his direction are a disgrace and a blight to God's work. How could we be wiser than God the Holy Spirit? Think of all the church decisions, both in personnel and finances, that are made without even ten minutes of serious prayer as to what the Holy Spirit might say.

> Who could ever possibly direct the affairs of the Christian church better than the Holy Spirit? If he gave specific instructions for the work back then, what verse in the Bible says he doesn't do it now?

No Bible doctrines, precious and vital as they are to us, can replace this kind of daily, specific leading by the Spirit of God. The leaders in Antioch could have read the whole Old Testament, inspired by God as it is, and yet never have known that the Holy Spirit wanted to send out Paul and Barnabas specifically. It took a direct intervention by the Spirit to get God's work going God's way.

Jesus said, "The harvest is plentiful but the workers are few. Ask the Lord of the harvest, therefore, to send out workers into his harvest field" (Matthew 9:37–38). In our churches today we have lots of critics and lots of people who like to discuss things—but not too many workers. Notice, though, that the directive is to pray that the Lord of the harvest will raise up and identify needed laborers.

Beyond Volunteerism

Neither emotional appeals for committed volunteers nor all the seminaries in the world can ever replace God's ordained method of divinely called laborers. Barnabas and Saul did not "volunteer." Neither were they voted in by some council in Antioch. Rather, they were summoned by a message from heaven. The Spirit himself appointed them.

I am not interested in debating *how* the Holy Spirit speaks. He certainly uses more than one way. I want to stay focused on the fact that the Spirit is alive, not dead, and that he *does* speak.

Yes, I know that some unscrupulous preachers today claim that "the Lord told me" when no such thing occurred. Others will say, "I just got a 'word' that ten people in this audience are supposed to give a thousand dollars each in the offering." This can be just a scam to raise money, and if the Lord really told them that, why didn't he reveal the people's names as well so we could get on with the meeting? Such behavior is an abomination. Jeremiah 23 holds harsh words for these charlatans:

> "I am against the prophets who wag their own tongues and yet declare, 'The LORD declares.' Indeed, I am against those who prophesy false dreams," declares the LORD. "They tell them and lead my people astray with their reckless lies, yet I did not send or appoint them....
>
> "This is what the LORD says: ... I will surely forget you and cast you out of my presence along with the city I gave to you and your fathers. I will bring upon you everlasting disgrace—everlasting shame that will not be forgotten" (vv. 31–32, 38–39).

What a scathing rebuke from God to all those who hide their greed and lust for power behind "Thus saith the Lord." Interestingly, this kind of abomination is almost always linked to dollar bills. Peter, in contrast, said, "Silver or gold I do not have" (Acts 3:6), but he certainly had something powerful from God. Today in certain circles, we have the opposite— spiritually empty but flashy preachers living like millionaires while they fleece the people with gimmicks that even the ungodly see through. Why not, rather, do as the apostle Paul did and simply present the need (see 2 Corinthians 8–9), trusting God to pour out a spirit of liberality upon his people?

But notice that even Jeremiah's condemnation of the false prophets came in the form of a *true* word from the Lord to his faithful prophet. God *is speaking* against those who prophesy reckless lies without inspiration from him. Satan is still trying today to move us away from the genuine working of the Spirit by the distraction and discouragement of phonies and frauds.

Once the Antioch leaders had received direction from the Holy Spirit, they did not immediately jump up to call the travel agent for Barnabas and Saul. According to Acts 13:3, they engaged in *more* fasting and prayer. Then "they placed their hands on them and sent them off." What consecration and devotion to the will and ways of God!

This devotion resulted in a wonderful cooperation between the church leadership and the activity of the Spirit, as we see in verse 4: "The two of them, *sent on their way by the Holy Spirit*, went down to Seleucia and sailed from there to Cyprus." The commissioning of the church was merely the outward expression of the divine commissioning.

I believe that if we could only hear better with spiritual ears today, we would hear a great cry from God the Holy Spirit over the roofs of our churches, district offices, seminaries, denominational headquarters, and mission agencies saying, "Listen to me! Hear me! I have a plan for you. I know how my work should be run. Stop everything for a while and listen for my voice."

SHOWDOWN TIME

Soon Barnabas and Saul (now renamed Paul) arrived on the Mediterranean island of Cyprus and began working their way across it, preaching this new gospel about a crucified Savior who rose again from the dead. In time they arrived in a city called Paphos.

What kind of open door did this Spirit-filled, Spirit-led pair discover? A Roman government official named Sergius Paulus invited them to come see him. What a great opportunity ... except that the official had an attendant in the room, an occultist named Elymas, who contradicted everything they said.

Opportunity and *opposition*: The two words start with the same set of letters, and they often travel together. We need never be discouraged when God opens a door to do something for him and we meet opposition almost immediately. This kind of thing happens all the time; it goes with the territory. What did we think Satan would do, anyway—cheer us on?

Opportunity and *opposition*: The two words start with the same set of letters, and they often travel together.

It was at this dramatic moment that "Paul, filled with the Holy Spirit" (v. 9), took charge. Luke's wording here is a carbon copy of his earlier description about Peter before the Sanhedrin (Acts 4:8), which we saw earlier in this book. Both of these showdowns resulted in a fresh impartation of Holy Spirit power.

In five high-voltage sentences Paul expressed keen spiritual discernment and strongly rebuked the sorcerer: "You are a child of the devil and an enemy of everything that is right! You are full of all kinds of deceit and trickery. Will you never stop perverting the right ways of the Lord? Now the hand of the Lord is against you. You are going to be blind, and for a time you will be unable to see the light of the sun" (Acts 13:10–11).

How strange this sounds to our modern ears. We would probably remind Paul that he was a guest in Sergius Paulus' house. He needed to remain polite and say the diplomatic thing. What kind of Christian was he, anyway? Isn't God a God of love? But the Spirit knows exactly what is appropriate for every situation, and in this case it was a bold rebuke despite the awkward circumstances.

Notice that Paul had absolutely no preparation for this. Nothing told him in advance that he would have to deal with a wizard that day. Once the showdown started, he didn't even consult with Barnabas. Instead, he was spiritually equipped and led by the faithful Spirit of God, who had gotten him into this situation in the first place! Having sent him out on the trip, the Spirit now gave him exactly what to say and do.

Within seconds Elymas began to stagger, groan pitifully, and stretch out his arms for support. The room erupted in gasps. The debate was over. Sergius Paulus became a believer in Christ that day, "for he was amazed at the teaching about the Lord" (v. 12). Who wouldn't yield to the Lord when the *teaching* was backed up by such a demonstration of the Spirit's power?

You may think that this kind of confrontation with the power of darkness occurred only in Bible times, or perhaps today in faraway jungles—but certainly not in sophisticated America. If so, then I should introduce you to Marissa Cunningham, a polished and articulate attorney in our church who works for a personal-injury firm in downtown Manhattan. Like Sergius Paulus, she is bright, intelligent, and capable.

About five years ago, while still in law school at Rutgers, Marissa found herself at loose ends due to some reversals in her life: a divorce, the stress of raising her daughter, Gianina, alone, and especially her inability to find a summer internship, which cast a cloud over her future road toward graduation. She didn't know where to turn. The Catholicism of her childhood back in Panama was no longer a force in her life; neither was the Eckankar religion that she had been exposed to since age twelve.

Marissa felt empty. Soon a vague sense of spiritual gloom settled over her. At times the horrible thought of ending her life would tantalize her, although she was normally an optimistic person. Would she really make it through law school and be able to start her professional career, or was everything going to fall apart? Clouds of depression blocked out any rays of light from her soul.

One day while walking along Fourth Avenue in Brooklyn to pay a telephone bill, Marissa saw a familiar sign on a storefront: *BOTANICA*. This, she knew, was a fortune-telling parlor based on Santeria, a form of Caribbean witchcraft. She peered in the window and saw that the waiting room was crowded.

She walked in and asked a few questions. "Oh, yes, our *curandero* is excellent," they said, referring to the witch doctor. "I'm sure he'll be able to help you." Marissa made an appointment for Wednesday.

When the time came, she entered the consultation room to meet a stocky man in his mid-forties. He invited her to sit down. Before long, he was telling her a number of specific events from her past life. Marissa was impressed—especially when he mentioned that she had a sharp pain in her left shoulder. That was absolutely true. He identified one of her friends by name and said this person had performed black magic against Marissa. And of course, he would be willing to help reverse the curse, for a price.

If she would come back on Friday with ninety dollars in cash, he would lead her through a cleansing ritual. They would take a chicken, rub it against Marissa's body "to get the scent," and then kill it. Draining the blood, he would take it to a cemetery for burial. This, he assured her, would be the answer she needed.

Marissa was repulsed by the idea, especially since as a vegetarian she opposed the killing of animals for any reason. Something didn't seem right here. Still, if this would really solve her problem and free her spirits, perhaps she should go along, she thought.

She went home and discussed the idea with friends. "Well, if it helps your situation," people said, "it's probably worth a try."

In the past Marissa had visited our church once or twice for a special occasion such as Easter. Now, in her uncertainty, she decided to stop by our office the next day. "I need to speak with a pastor—someone with a lot of power!" she insisted. As it turned out, no pastors were available, and Marissa got to speak instead with a woman on our staff named Elsie Lherisson. Soon Elsie, who just "happened" to have grown up in Haiti and knew all about Santeria, was telling Marissa that the goodness of God was much stronger than her personal distress and that God alone had the power to deliver her. She invited Marissa to come to our Foundation Bible Study class that evening.

"Well, I don't know about that," Marissa replied skeptically. But as the hours passed, her apprehension about the next day's ritual with the chicken increased, to the point that she returned to the church for the class. She arrived late, the room was crowded, and the only remaining seat was next to a man in ripped jeans—certainly not someone of the social standing Marissa preferred. She had to force herself to take the seat.

At the evening's halfway break, a conversation began. The man introduced himself as John. "So what brought you here?" he asked. Soon Marissa was telling about going to the *botanica* and the unusual things that had happened there.

Opening his Bible to Ephesians 6, John read, "For our struggle is not against flesh and blood, but against the rulers, against the authorities, against the powers of this dark world and against the spiritual forces of evil in the heavenly realms."

He then said, "Satan does have real power. That's why that man could tell you about your past, the pain in your shoulder, and everything. But there's someone greater, with much more power, than him."

"Who is that?" Marissa asked.

"Jesus."

By the end of the night, Marissa felt that these people truly cared about her. They didn't treat her as if she was a nut for going to a fortune-teller; they wanted to give her a better answer. Soon she found herself in a circle with John, the teacher and his wife, and a couple of others. "God is good, and he wants good things for you," someone said. "We're going to say a prayer now, and it will be life-changing for you. You don't have to kill a chicken to solve your problem. The truth is, the necessary blood was already spilled—two thousand years ago, when Jesus died on the cross for you. He loves you, he cares about you, and he can set you free." Then came a sincere prayer for forgiveness and cleansing, and Marissa stepped from darkness into light.

Amid her tears, she heard the leader say, "Now you don't have to fear any spirits or curses, Marissa. Your name is now written in the Book of Life in heaven. Jesus lives within you. He loves you and will protect you."

WALKING IN THE LIGHT

Marissa went home that Thursday night with a small seed of faith in her heart. The next day she skipped her appointment at the *botanica*. Instead, on Sunday she walked with her daughter to our church.

Nearing the building on a side street, she glanced at a blue van in the traffic and saw a man staring at her from the passenger-side window. Her heart jumped as she realized who it was: the *curandero!* Marissa caught her breath. Here she was, heading for church, and in that moment the very henchman of evil had his eye on her, scrutinizing her every move.

She kept walking steadily and was relieved to step inside the doors of the church. On Tuesday night she returned to the prayer meeting. When I invited people to come forward for special prayer, she responded. Kneeling in the middle of the aisle with others, she began to weep. "I just knew God loved me and was reaching out for me," she remembers. "I had to follow him. At that point I resolved that there would be no turning back. I had to find out more about Jesus and his love."

We discipled Marissa in the subsequent months. Today she is a solid believer and a wonderful asset to our church.

Gospel work in our day must be more than just little stories, doctrinal presentations, and polite lectures. It must carry a sense of God's living power. It must show a living Holy Spirit who is still active on the earth. We hear endlessly about the growing menace of the occult and Satan's hold on people. But if Satan is alive and working in the earth, can we not expect the living, all-powerful Spirit of God to work also?

> **Gospel work in our day must be more than just little stories, doctrinal presentations, and polite lectures. It must carry a sense of God's living power.**

That is what the author of Hebrews indicated when he said the message of salvation "was first announced by the Lord ... [and] God also testified to it by signs, wonders and various miracles, and gifts of the Holy Spirit distributed according to his will" (2:3–4). In other words, the antidote to satanic schemes is twofold: the Word of God and a demonstration of Holy Spirit power.

When strangers visit our churches today, they need to *see* something happening that reinforces the message of salvation. They need to meet the reclaimed alcoholic, the reunited family, the former homosexual who has been turned around, the sick person who was healed—*something* that bears witness to a living, powerful Savior.

We must pray as never before, "Lord, come down to us and *work with* the word we preach. Stretch out your hand as we deliver the message you gave us." We must rearrange our busy personal and church schedules to make time for what the church at Antioch did when "they ministered to the Lord" (Acts 13:2 KJV). In our times of waiting, prayer, and fasting, God will faithfully respond to our need for more of him.

In *Fresh Wind, Fresh Fire* I told about Daniel Nash, the obscure man who locked himself away in prayer whenever the great evangelist Charles G. Finney went out to preach. The very last letter Nash wrote before his death in 1831 contains this moving passage:

> Since you were here I have been thinking of prayer— particularly of praying for the Holy Ghost and its descent. It seems to me I have always limited God in this request. . . . I have never felt, till since you left us, that I might rationally ask for the whole influence of the Spirit to come down; not only on individuals, but on a whole people, region, country, and world. On Saturday I set myself to do this, and the devil was very angry with me, yesterday for it. I am now convinced, it is my duty and privilege, and the duty of every other Christian, to pray for as much of the Holy Spirit as came down on the day of Pentecost, and a great deal more. I know not why we may not ask for the entire and utmost influence of the Spirit to come down, and, asking in faith, see the full answer.[3]

Carol and I, along with our whole pastoral staff, were convinced long ago that our ministry in Brooklyn is absolutely hopeless without the Holy Spirit. We have no talent or ability in ourselves that will do the job. Only the Spirit of God can help us make a difference for Jesus Christ.

The Spirit *is here on the earth*, waiting to respond to our longing for him to come in fresh power upon us. Then we will appreciate with a new depth of meaning the old chorus we often sing in our church:

> *God is moving by his Spirit,*
> *Moving in all the earth;*
> *Signs and wonders when God moveth;*
> *Move, O Lord, in me.*[4]

TEN

Joy and a Whole Lot More

IF YOU WALK INTO any Christian bookstore these days, you will find an abundance of titles just trying to get believers out of their "funk." Depression appears to be a major tide in the Christian community. Researcher George Barna says today's churchgoers are gulping down almost as many antidepressant drugs as their secular neighbors.

This is not a very good billboard advertisement for Jesus, who said, "I have come that they may have life, and have it to the full. . . . Ask and you will receive, and your joy will be complete" (John 10:10; 16:24).

But instead of being known as a joyous people, we often surrender to a victim mentality. I have heard repeatedly over the years, "Because such-and-such happened to me when I was growing up . . . because I was mistreated in a former church . . . because of all the pressures in my life that nobody else can feel . . . I'm entitled to sulk and pout." A lot of pressure on pastors today comes from trying to deal with people who feel perpetually misunderstood or mistreated.

All this is in sharp contrast to the mental and spiritual state of the new Christians in Antioch of Pisidia, a city Paul visited on his first missionary journey. Luke summarizes the state of that newborn church in words we almost never hear today: "And the disciples were filled with joy and with the Holy Spirit" (Acts 13:52). Notice that this succinct, twelve-word description focuses on the spiritual condition of those recently won to Christ. How many church leaders even think along these lines when discussing the work of God? Instead, it's all about attendance numbers, the physical plant, and the budget. I'm afraid we're missing the point.

At first glance you might be tempted to assume that the Antioch people were riding just an initial burst of enthusiasm following salvation. They were fired up in the beginning, but they probably settled down within a few months, right?

In response to Paul's initial ministry in the synagogue, some people had begun to open up to the gospel. The apostles "talked with them and urged them to *continue in the grace of God*" (v. 43). The text doesn't say anything about giving these people twenty rules of Christian conduct or asking them to make a series of promises and commitments to "live right." Instead, they highlighted the fact that God was working in their lives through the gracious influences of the Holy Spirit. This was the essence of the New Covenant, and so the new converts should continue in openness and trust.

GOD AT WORK

Grace is a rich and multifaceted word in the New Testament. One of its primary meanings is God doing for us, by the Holy Spirit, what we cannot do for ourselves. Whether we are overcoming sinful habits, preaching, teaching a class, leading a choir, or being a godly spouse in the home, we cannot succeed without the grace of God. As Paul wrote in Philippians 2:13, "It is God *who works in you* to will and to act according to his good purpose." Notice that we need God's help not just in the *doing* part but also in *willing* to walk in his ways.

The apostles wanted the believers at Antioch to let the living God continue working in their lives, their relationships, their endeavors. This highlights the fact that the very essence of Christian living is supernatural. Those who had received forgiveness of sin had also been given the Holy Spirit, who would now carry on the work of salvation in their souls.

> **Many of us are tempted to fall into ... "Old Testament Christianity." The very phrase is an oxymoron, I admit, and no wonder it doesn't work.**

This is the antidote to what many of us are tempted to fall into, which is "Old Testament Christianity." The very phrase is an oxymoron, I admit, and no wonder it doesn't work. We seem not to understand the radical difference of the New Covenant. Hebrews 8:7–10 says,

> For if there had been nothing wrong with that first covenant, no place would have been sought for another. But God found fault with the people and said:
>
> "The time is coming, declares the Lord,
>   when I will make a new covenant
> with the house of Israel
>   and with the house of Judah.
> It will *not be* like the covenant
>   I made with their forefathers
> when I took them by the hand
>   to lead them out of Egypt,
> because they did not remain faithful to my covenant,
>   and I turned away from them,
>   declares the Lord.

This is the covenant I will make with the house of Israel
    after that time, declares the Lord.
I will put my laws *in their minds*
    and write them *on their hearts*.
I will be their God,
    and they will be my people."

The problem with the Old Covenant was not with God
but rather with humanity, which was so ruined by sin that
people were unable to keep God's holy commands no matter
how hard they tried. Thus, "it will not be like the covenant I
made with their forefathers." There was the need for a whole
new arrangement on a totally different basis.

This is far more than a set of schematic drawings on a
theological chalkboard. To fully understand the New
Covenant, we must understand the Holy Spirit and what he
does. The Old Covenant, which was characterized by the
Law given to Moses, was a set of external commands. The
New Covenant is about Christ's atoning death and resurrec-
tion from the grave, followed by the sending of the Holy
Spirit to work *inside* us in grace and power.

No one disagreed with the content of the old commands;
they had been written with the finger of God himself. But no
matter how many times people came up to the altar and
promised to try to obey, they repeatedly fell short. Thank
God that he sent the Holy Spirit at last to bring about real
change *within* us who have received Christ as Savior and
Lord.

When God puts his laws in our minds by the Spirit
(Hebrews 8:10), he reshapes our very thinking. When he
writes them on our hearts, he affects our very springs of
desire and longing. This is the only way Christian living goes
forward.

Otherwise, we are doomed to keep coming back to God saying, "I messed up again. Run those laws by me once more, if you will, and I'll promise to get it right this time...." How many Christians today are striving to show their gratitude to Jesus, the one who brought the New Covenant to earth, by living in an Old Covenant way? It is absolutely futile. It is the opposite of Ezekiel 11:19–20, where the Lord promises, "*I will give them an undivided heart and put a new spirit in them; I will remove from them their heart of stone and give them a heart of flesh. Then they will follow my decrees and be careful to keep my laws. They will be my people, and I will be their God.*"

The power to be different comes from heaven, not from our own strength. The Holy Spirit was given, as his name implies, so that we can live a holy life for God. Any other source or system, no matter how religious-sounding, is a fraud and leads to defeat due to the fleshly impulses of our sinful nature. The Holy Spirit's power is not an *option* for those who desperately want to be like Christ; he is the only answer. We must get delivered from the idea so prevalent around us that Christianity begins with a supernatural new birth, sin is erased, the conscience is cleansed—but then it's up to us to try real hard to be good and obey God's commands. No, it is God's work from beginning to end. Just as forgiveness can *only* come through Christ's work on Calvary, daily living for the Lord can *only* be done through the Spirit. That is what the wonderful verse means when it declares that "the salvation of the righteous"—all of it— "comes from the LORD" (Psalm 37:39).

> The power to be different comes from heaven, not from our own strength. The Holy Spirit was given, as his name implies, so that we can live a holy life for God.

The Word That Divides

All this serves to show how Paul and Barnabas started off the new believers in Antioch. Within a week, "almost the whole city gathered to hear the word of the Lord" (Acts 13:44). It seemed that a great awakening was under way.

But once again, trouble raised its head. "When the Jews saw the crowds, they were filled with jealousy and talked abusively against what Paul was saying" (v. 45). This tells us that even preachers of the caliber of the apostle Paul didn't win every person to Christ. Some listeners turned him down flat and even began to harass him. And these opponents were not just on the fringe of society; they were "women of high standing and the leading men of the city" (v. 50).

I attended a conference once where a teacher who seemed bold and full of faith declared that "Paul never left a city until everyone was won to Christ." Young, sincere ministers were impressed and took notes diligently. They would have done better to remember the first question for assessing any sermon (or any book): *Is this taught in the Bible? What does Scripture say?*

This speaker was obviously confused in his attempt to describe "power evangelism." In fact, the gospel message will always attract opposition and rejection, whether in Brooklyn or in Bangkok. This is true even when God works miracles. Remember that in the cities where Jesus did his most amazing wonders, the response was often disappointing. "Woe to you, Korazin! Woe to you, Bethsaida!" he said. "For if the miracles that were performed in you had been performed in Tyre and Sidon, they would have repented long ago, sitting in sackcloth and ashes" (Luke 10:13).

The Word of God has a dividing characteristic about it; Hebrews calls it a "double-edged sword" for a reason. As Paul the realist wrote a few years after these events in Antioch, "For we are to God the aroma of Christ among those who are being saved and those who are perishing. To the one we are the smell of death; to the other, the fragrance of life. And who is equal to such a task?" (2 Corinthians 2:15–16). But this fact should never dampen our enthusiasm to do God's work. Great harvests are still awaiting us as we preach the message of Christ with the Spirit's help.

> The gospel message will always attract opposition and rejection, whether in Brooklyn or in Bangkok. This is true even when God works miracles.

I suppose that some preachers, if faced with a mounting campaign of slurs and insults from the power brokers in city hall, would second-guess themselves. *What did I say wrong? How can I win them back? Maybe I need to change the message. Did God really send me here? Maybe we could put on some kind of drama that wouldn't focus so much on the name of Jesus. They don't seem ready yet for the gospel. That's what gets us in so much hot water....*

Not Paul and Barnabas. With boldness from the Holy Spirit they declared to the Jews, "We had to speak the word of God to you first. Since you reject it and do not consider yourselves worthy of eternal life, we now turn to the Gentiles" (Acts 13:46).

What a difference from the "market mentality" we have in the church today, always pandering to the wishes and preferences of certain audiences. Too many pastors have become like the host of a late-night talk show, analyzing the Nielsen ratings to see if their routines are keeping them ahead of the competition. What would brave Paul and Barnabas say with regard to our modern, effeminate preaching?

You will never convince me that today we are smarter, more hip, or better at "relating" than the old crude style. If that is so, where are the spiritual results? Where are the supernaturally changed converts, the mass baptisms, the passionate prayer meetings, the hunger for holiness? Where is all our cleverness getting us? Is America getting more godly with each passing decade?

The Gentiles in Antioch, of course, were pleased with the apostles' announcement, and in just a short time "the word of the Lord spread through the whole region" (v. 49). But that did not prevent the upper-class enemies from having their way. Soon they managed to kick Paul and Barnabas out of town.

> **You will never convince me that today we are smarter, more hip, or better at "relating" than the old crude style. If that is so, where are the spiritual results?**

This left the common people of Antioch in a vulnerable spot. They didn't have clout in the halls of government. Their faith in Jesus Christ was still new and tender. And their spiritual leaders were now gone, evicted in a cloud of controversy. No literature was left for them to study. They had no legal standing or steepled building. Opposition was strong.

How do you think they felt? Apprehensive? Abandoned? Uncertain? Depressed? Did someone say, "Let's just forget about following Jesus. I can't afford to lose my job, you know. It's not safe. Maybe we got carried away . . ."?

This is the setting for Luke's amazing report: "And as for the disciples, they were more and more filled with joy and with the Holy Spirit!" (v. 52 Weymouth). What a rebuke to our modern rationalization for sour spirits and depressed attitudes. If these new believers could so rejoice in the God of their salvation, then what could be *our* problem?

But that's what the Holy Spirit is all about. He can overcome hostile environments and fill us again and again with joy. He helps us swim against the strongest tide.

JOY IN THE HARDEST TIMES

Many Bible readers do not realize that this Antioch group was one of the churches in the province of Galatia to whom Paul later wrote this familiar passage: "The fruit of the Spirit is love, *joy*, peace, patience, kindness, goodness, faithfulness, gentleness and self-control. Against such things there is no law.... Since we live by the Spirit, let us keep in step with the Spirit" (Galatians 5:22–23, 25).

These nine wonderful traits are produced not by you or me but by the Holy Spirit. If someone calls you a *loving* person, the credit is not yours. It is rather the result of the Spirit living within you and producing Christlike character. The same is true for *joy* in the face of setbacks, *peace* in the face of trouble, and all the rest of the list.

If we have been born again by the Spirit, the only way to grow to be more like Jesus is by the power of the same Spirit. As we "keep in step with the Spirit," following his motions along the daily road, he will gradually conform us into the image of God's Son.

One of the soloists in our choir is a woman in her mid-thirties named Robin Giles. She works as a secretary and lives by herself not far from the church. Carol and I deeply appreciate her sincere and gracious spirit. The fruits of peace, kindness, and gentleness are especially evident in her life along with the joy of the Lord. When Robin sings, that joy is wonderfully communicated no matter the song.

That is truly amazing, given the vicious atmosphere in which she grew up in Cleveland. Back when Robin was born to an unmarried twenty-one-year-old, it was obviously a "mistake." Her mother hated Robin's father and lived in a state of perpetual rage toward the daughter she was now stuck with.

"I grew up in a house of fear," Robin says. From early years she was yelled at, slapped about, and beaten. "I never remember a single hug or a kiss. The words I heard most often were 'You're stupid!' 'Everything you touch, you mess up.' 'I wish you were dead!'"

Along the way, Robin's mother married an older man, a crane operator, whose presence helped to temper the eruptions in the home. But whenever the stepfather was gone, Robin feared for her life. More than once she was threatened with a gun. One day when she was nine and her mother began to berate her, the little girl fled to a large closet.

"Come out of there right now!" her mother shrieked.

Robin stayed put, holding her breath.

Her mother's yelling subsided, and she seemed to walk away. Robin peeked out to learn whether the storm had passed. Edging out of the closet, she looked toward the kitchen—and saw her mother heating up a metal pancake turner over the gas range.

Suddenly the woman turned and came flying in her direction. Robin ran for the safety of the closet again, but didn't get there in time. Soon the hot metal was searing itself against her arm.

"Momma, please!" she cried out. "Don't hurt me!"

Her mother finally stopped the attack. In a few minutes she got out a roll of gauze and began bandaging the wound. But still she snarled, "See what you made me do?!"

In fact, Robin was the opposite of an aggravating child. She made straight A's in school, kept quiet, read a lot, and tried her best to please. But nothing could tame her mother's rage.

A few days later in school, the gym teacher asked Robin, "Oooh, what happened to your arm?" The little girl ached to tell the truth, but was afraid. She mumbled an excuse.

By the time she turned twelve, Robin's stepfather had suffered his second heart attack and died, leaving her unprotected. When her mother caught her one summer night sitting on the front porch and talking to a boy out on the sidewalk, she unleashed the most brutal beating to date. With a doubled-up electrical cord she lashed Robin until welts appeared on her head and open gashes bled from her arm. When she was done, her only words were "Now go wash the dishes."

It was the final straw. Robin ran away to a girlfriend's house, staying two weeks. But when she learned that a warrant had been issued for her arrest, she turned herself in, with high hopes that the authorities would listen to her story and help her. To her shock, she was instead locked up in a juvenile detention center for three months. The bitterness began to grow inside her heart.

What would you expect this young lady to become in life? Given this horrendous start, this overwhelming rejection from the one person who's supposed to love you no matter what—how would you rate her chances? This is the typical kind of case that comes to New York City as a runaway and ends up in the bus terminal on Eighth Avenue and Forty-first Street. Drug dealers and pimps spot them in a second. These human predators easily con them into trusting them and have them hooked on drugs or selling their bodies in no time at all.

REMOVING THE STING

The next eleven years for Robin were a rough road of self-doubt, depression, inner seething at the unfairness of life, irresponsible relationships, and even a suicide attempt. Despite the help of a godly foster home during her high school years, "I had a chip on my shoulder," she admits. "I felt I had a right to be angry." Not until she was in her mid-twenties did a friend at work invite her to church, guiding her to a Savior who truly loved her and could be trusted. When she moved to New York a few years later, her pastor in Cleveland recommended our church, and it has been our joy to have her here.

She is a walking example of Jesus' ability to set the captive free and to heal the brokenhearted. "God has taken the sting out of my past," she says. "For so long the memories of my mother's behavior kept me from experiencing abundant life. But then I realized one day that the Lord had changed my heart toward her. I had hated her for so long. God totally took that away."

The woman still will have nothing to do with her daughter. She refuses even to give Robin her current address in Cleveland. If Robin sends a message through a neighborhood friend, she may get a return phone call or she may not. The mother has never heard her daughter sing with our choir.

"But I'm still praying for her," says Robin. "And I'm looking forward to the day that she'll maybe meet someone and be led to the Lord at last.

God is stronger than any abuse. The Holy Spirit has the power to defuse the most raging resentment. He brings his power into the most troubled lives and produces something beautiful.

"In the meantime, God is so faithful. He has brought so many people in my life to be mothers and fathers to me. I'm doubly blessed."

I can tell you on the basis of twenty-eight years in the ministry that it is harder to repair this kind of damage to a person than to break the power of crack cocaine. Many would say Robin has every right to be bitter. What her mother did—and keeps doing—is absolutely dreadful. Robin Giles could have been a walking time bomb.

But God is stronger than any abuse. The Holy Spirit has the power to defuse the most raging resentment. He brings his power into the most troubled lives and produces something beautiful.

When we had Robin give her testimony in a Sunday night meeting, it happened to be the Fourth of July. She alluded to the holiday and said, "The Lord has given me freedom from *my* past, and I'm so thankful!" Then, as tears welled up in my eyes and many of those present, she sang the solo part for a choir song Carol had written back in 1987:

> *When all the strength you have is gone*
> *And friends that you've depended on*
> *Can't hear the cry you try to hide*
> *Or feel the pain you keep inside,*
> *All, all you really need is Jesus.*
>
> *When clouds arise and light grows dim,*
> *He calls on you to look to him.*
> *Your simple prayer will reach his heart,*
> *His perfect peace he will impart.*
> *All, all you really need is Jesus.*
>
> Chorus: *All that you need is Jesus,*
> *All that you need is God.*
> *Cast your every care on him who answers prayer.*
> *All that you need is God.*[1]

God declares to us that this "joy of the LORD is your strength" (Nehemiah 8:10). To walk in joylessness and despondency is by definition to forfeit our strength and vitality for the challenges of life we all face. But Jesus knows from his own human experience on earth that trials, pressures, and temptations exert a tremendous downward pull on our souls—and he is faithful. The Holy Spirit has been sent to lift up our heads, no matter the circumstances, and fulfill the word spoken by the prophet so long ago: "Gladness and joy will overtake them, and sorrow and sighing will flee away" (Isaiah 51:11).

ELEVEN

Through Many Hardships

IMAGINE, IF YOU WILL, that your telephone rings one day with astonishingly good news. A pleasant young voice says, "I'm a representative of Carol Joy Enterprises, and do you remember putting your name into a drawing last month in a store to win a month-long, all-expenses-paid vacation to the English countryside? Guess what—you're the winner!"

You might begin to scream and shout and dance around the room. "Are you serious?! Oh, my goodness, I can't believe it! I've never won anything in my life!"

Immediately your head would fill with images of the green, rolling hills you saw on the poster in the store ... the quaint little cottages with the thatched roofs ... the narrow cobblestone streets ... the sheep calmly grazing in the meadows ... the stone fences ... the delightful shops. Now it is all to be yours: a free package of airfare, lodging, food, and activities.

"Come to our offices tomorrow at 11 o'clock, and we'll give you the details," the representative continues. She quotes the address and then hangs up.

That night you can hardly sleep. You're going on a free vacation! By the next morning, your excitement is still strong.

When you sit down across the desk from the woman, she confirms the truth of the phone call the day before—yes, you've really won a month of leisure in England. She checks your identification and takes down essential data. Eventually she starts to explain the particulars.

"Okay, on May 17, you have a 7:40 p.m. flight out of Kennedy airport, so you'll need to be there by 5:30," she says.

"Kennedy airport?" you ask with a frown. "I don't like Kennedy. It's really hard to get there from where I live, especially in the middle of the evening rush hour. I thought you said I was getting a free vacation in England."

"Yes—well, it all starts by catching a flight from Kennedy," she replies. "You'll have to wait in several lines and have your luggage checked and show your passport, and then when the plane finally takes off, you'll be flying all night to London. You probably won't be able to sleep very well in those little seats, but that's just the way it is. . . ."

"I don't like the sound of this at all," you complain. "What if the plane goes down in the ocean?"

The woman rolls her eyes. "Look, it's not going to go down."

"Well, I get nervous in an airplane."

She ignores you. "And then when you get to Heathrow Airport in London—"

"Wait a minute! You said I was going to the English countryside."

"Yes, well, first you have to stand in a long line at the customs checkpoint in the airport. When you finally get up to the front, they'll ask you some questions and stamp your passport. Then you'll have to get your luggage and haul it out to the bus, which will take you into the city to catch the train. It's a three-hour train ride before you finally get to your hotel."

You're getting quite irritated now. "I don't want to do all that," you insist. "I just want to walk out of my house and go straight to the little English village."

At this point the woman would probably be ready to disqualify you and pick another winner!

THE HARD FACTS

We have all met more than a few Christians who expect their trip to heaven to be one smooth ride from the time they accepted Christ straight to the pearly gates—especially here in America, where the culture is overwhelmingly pleasure-oriented. As a result, believers in Christ have lost their bearings about what a godly life is all about. Unfortunately, a lot of gospel preaching adds to the problem, since it conveniently omits the hard facts of spiritual life.

> **More than a few Christians expect their trip to heaven to be one smooth ride from the time they accepted Christ straight to the pearly gates.**

We don't linger very long in passages such as this one, especially the parts I have put into italic:

> At Iconium Paul and Barnabas went as usual into the Jewish synagogue. There they spoke so effectively that a great number of Jews and Gentiles believed. *But the Jews who refused to believe stirred up the Gentiles and poisoned their minds against the brothers.* So Paul and Barnabas spent considerable time there, speaking boldly for the Lord, who confirmed the message of his grace by enabling them to do miraculous signs and wonders. *The people of the city were divided; some sided with the Jews, others with the apostles. There was a plot afoot among the Gentiles and Jews, together with their leaders, to mistreat them and stone them.* But they found out about it and fled to the Lycaonian cities of Lystra and Derbe and to

the surrounding country, where they continued to preach the good news (Acts 14:1–7).

In Lystra God enabled Paul to perform a marvelous miracle, the healing of a man crippled from birth. The crowd was amazed and began to think Paul and Barnabas were some of the Greek gods. But their fame was short-lived.

> *Then some Jews came from Antioch and Iconium and won the crowd over. They stoned Paul and dragged him outside the city, thinking he was dead.* But after the disciples had gathered around him, he got up and went back into the city (Acts 14:19–20).

The longer I live and the more people I talk to as a pastor, the more I find that life contains a lot of "stuff." People think the Christian life is going to be a breeze, and it's not. Trouble breaks loose in their lives, and all of a sudden they're crying, "Where is God? Nobody told me this was going to happen."

The advertising mentality so prevalent in the church is "We need to get more converts, so don't anybody say anything negative. Otherwise, they might not sign up." We're like car salesmen trying to point out the fancy features without mentioning the dubious crash-test ratings. A lot of preaching is not totally honest because the speaker is afraid he won't "close the deal."

Paul did not do this. Notice what happened immediately after his being battered into unconsciousness by the stoning. No doubt his wounds were still being treated, and yet—

> The next day he and Barnabas left for Derbe.
> They preached the good news in that city and won a large number of disciples. Then they returned to Lystra, Iconium and Antioch, strengthening the disciples and encouraging them to remain true to the

faith. *"We must go through many hardships to enter the kingdom of God,"* they said (Acts 14:19–22).

Why in the world would Paul go back to Lystra, of all places? You would think he would never want to see that town again, after the stoning. But he was greatly concerned about his converts and wanted to nurture them further. Included in his teaching about the rudiments of the Christian faith was the stark but honest statement that "we must go through many hardships to enter the kingdom of God." Not "we *might* . . ." but "we *must.* . . ."

The Greek word translated "hardships" means to break, crush, compress, squeeze. It signifies distress, pressure, a burden upon the spirit. Paul included this kind of honest teaching in every town where a church had sprung up. The believers in these churches had to keep in mind always that in the kingdom of God, hardship and persecution are par for the course. That's just the way it is.

Just because someone quotes a stirring Bible verse, or "takes authority" over his problem, or "rebukes Satan" doesn't mean the trial always melts away. To present that notion to new Christians is a terrible distortion of God's Word. Years later, near the end of his life, Paul referred back to the time of Acts 14 as he wrote to Timothy, "You, however, know all about my teaching, my way of life, my purpose, faith, patience, love, endurance, persecutions, sufferings—what kinds of things happened to me in Antioch, Iconium and Lystra, the persecutions I endured. Yet the Lord rescued me from all of them. *In fact, everyone who wants to live a godly life in Christ Jesus will be persecuted"* (2 Timothy 3:10–12).

No Free Ride

If the great apostle Paul said that persecution was inevitable (from personal experience, no less), who are we to think we will somehow avoid it?

Job's friend Eliphaz summed it up succinctly when he said, "Man is born to trouble as surely as sparks fly upward" (Job 5:7). Life on a sinful earth when you want to live for Jesus Christ involves even more challenges. We will be attacked by the devil—and that is not fun. But God permits testings and trials nonetheless. If you think there's a formula whereby you can avoid these things, you're wrong. The danger is that people who are not aware of the spiritual facts of life can get shaken up and think that something unusual is happening. They need to know that in spite of all the prayer and support and encouragement, they are still going to go through some "stuff" in this life.

Some of the pain we endure is emotional and can come from within our own family. A relative says, "So you've gotten religious, have you? What do you think you are—better than us now?" It hurts to hear those kinds of words.

We have seen new converts in our church often face this kind of thing. When they were partying all night and doing drugs, no one seemed bothered. But now that they are following Christ and coming to church regularly, it sets off a reaction from their own flesh and blood. "Why do you always have to be in church? What are you, some kind of fanatic?" Prior to this they didn't care even if the person was stoned out of his mind.

It is vital that we not be misled. That is what Paul was concerned about upon leaving the Thessalonian believers after just three short weeks. "We sent Timothy ... to strengthen and encourage you in your faith, so that no one would be unsettled *by these trials*. You know quite well that *we were destined for them*. In fact, when we were with you, we kept telling you that *we would be persecuted*. And it turned out that way, as you well know" (1 Thessalonians 3:2–4).

Compare these parts of God's Word with the terrible deception being practiced in some quarters today. People are told that when you learn to "make the promises work for you," you will live on spiritual Easy Street. No trials, no suffering, only big cars, big bank accounts—that's God's plan for every one of his children. The churches that teach this could be indicted for false advertising.

I heard about one "faith" preacher who needed medical care and, with embarrassment, checked himself into a hospital under an alias so no one would find out he wasn't "claiming the victory." He gave orders to refuse all phone calls, taking every measure possible that the word not get out about his illness.

Another teacher of this persuasion has said that poor Paul didn't really understand "positive confession" and the "word of faith," or he would never have gone through all his problems. Imagine! This "poor Paul" wrote a great part of the New Testament. If he wasn't divinely inspired when he wrote of inevitable trouble and suffering for the believer, *where else* was he mistaken? Given this kind of false teaching, we might soon have no New Testament at all.

So many folks love to pick and choose their verses, hanging on to their favorites while sweeping under the rug the parts that don't agree with their carnal desires. The prosperity teachers are very clever; they have made an industry out of telling people what they *want* to hear. But God says there is a curse on anyone who adds to or takes away any part of his sacred Word.

The apostles were careful to do two things well:

1. *Correctly handle the word of truth* (2 Timothy 2:15). They did not just snatch up an individual verse and make it their only theme. They interpreted Scripture faithfully.

2. *Proclaim the whole will of God* (Acts 20:27). They delivered the full scope of God's truth, not just what people wanted to hear.

A man from New Jersey called our church in Brooklyn not long ago to ask for a counseling appointment.

"What is the problem that you want to talk about?" Pastor Frank O'Neill, one of our associate pastors, asked.

"My wife and I are having financial problems, and I want some help."

"Well, how about going to your own church there in New Jersey? Wouldn't it be best to talk to your own pastor?"

No, no, no, he couldn't do that, the man said. The leaders there had already instructed him that problems such as his had to be dealt with by a positive confession, and that's all it took. He had already tried this approach. "I just want you to know," he went on, slipping into what sounded like a mantra, "that my wife and I have spoken the word of faith—and *we have no debts! I repeat, we have no debts! The bills are NOT there! The creditors are NOT after us! We speak to this situation in the name of the Lord!*"

Pastor O'Neill didn't know whether to laugh or cry. What the man was saying was ludicrous, but it was also very sad.

"So then, uh, tell me again why you're calling us?" he asked quietly.

"Well, we have no debts, we have no bills," the man repeated, "and we are victorious in the Lord. But I just want to ask you one thing: *Would it be a sin to file for bankruptcy?*"

Talk about confusion!

Sometimes we go through troubles that are merely of our own doing. We are simply reaping what we sowed.

Rough Start

At other times we can be full of the Holy Spirit and in the center of God's will—and still, like Paul, get locked up in jail. If the Master whom we follow was cruicified, on what basis do we think we will escape all trouble? If we speak the truth as he did, and as Paul did, not everyone is going to be pleased.

> **If the Master whom we follow was crucified, on what basis do we think we will escape all trouble?**

I am finding out that in Christian conferences and meetings today, not everyone is open to the Word of God. Many have their own agendas and traditions, which they dearly cherish even though they contradict or deny Scripture. It seems their goal is not so much to grow in Christ as it is to maintain the status quo at all costs.

How dare anyone even hint that God desires to change some part of their lives or church ministries! They bristle at preaching that confronts them with God's promise of power from on high, or the kind of church we find in the New Testament.

Lately I have been confronted by a few angry people who were annoyed by my preaching. When I sincerely asked them to show me where I misspoke according to Scripture, they had no real response. I had apparently not mishandled the Bible but only stepped on their toes.

For example, I recently learned that some pastors have gone to using video clips from filthy, R-rated movies to "illustrate" truth in their "contemporary" services right in God's house! All that does is endorse the kind of immoral entertainment that is plaguing the spiritual lives of thousands. And it can stir up fleshly impulses in countless more. All of this is, of course, excused under the guise of effectively communicating in a contemporary manner. If you are bothered by any of these methods, many will laugh you off as maladjusted to the modern world.

But I have a simple question: Would Jesus sit and comfortably watch such garbage? Better yet, how grieved is the Holy Spirit who dwells within us and whose name is holy?

Aren't God's Word and the Holy Spirit enough to hold the people's attention and work wonders as they did two thousand years ago? Has God run out of steam? The angels must cry when they see such compromise and unbelief. How can men and women of God not lift their voices against such subtle apostasy, no matter the personal consequences?

> **Aren't God's Word and the Holy Spirit enough to hold the people's attention and work wonders as they did two thousand years ago? Has God run out of steam?**

When people react bitterly, it pains me personally, for I want to be liked and accepted like anyone else. But how can one close his eyes to divine truth that the people of God have embraced for hundreds of years? How can one ignore scriptural principles that have spawned spiritual revivals and shaken whole nations? We have forgotten the warning that says, "Do not move an ancient boundary stone set up by your forefathers" (Proverbs 22:28).

What many are defending as "diversity of ministry" is really a departure from the Word of God and the person of the Holy Spirit. The world and its carnal thinking have so invaded the church that we have been "evangelized," and we don't even know it. But how inconsequential is my emotional discomfort compared with people who have truly experienced the depths of the verse that says, "If we endure, we will also reign with him" (2 Timothy 2:12).

When I read these kinds of Scriptures, I think about Denise Tsikudo, a short little woman in our church who came to the Lord in early 1993. At that time she was a single mother with two daughters; she had no particular religious background other than a stint in witchcraft. Her recreational drug use had increased, and so had her binge drinking, to two or three times a week, which created a sense of depression. It was this dilemma that nudged her toward coming to church, where she soon gave her heart to Christ.

She stopped all drinking. She quit chain-smoking. But did everything run smoothly thereafter?

Within just a few months, while she was still a baby believer, Denise suffered the sudden loss of her mother. There was no warning; Denise found her dead on the bathroom floor of her house in Bedford-Stuyvesant, where she lived alone.

Once the shock subsided, Denise had to sort out her mother's legal affairs, a complicated task. Disagreements arose among the relatives at certain points. What should be done with the house? Denise's aunt urged her to take over the property, even though it was in a high-risk area and even though she had little spare money to put into taxes and upkeep.

Her sisters and brothers rebuffed her, now that she had "gotten religious." Her friends who had been quite willing to stay up all night with her doing drugs were critical of how much time she was now spending in church.

At the end of July that year, she signed up for what we call our Foundation Bible Class, an introductory course in the Christian faith. The first Thursday night session went well, she remembers. She returned home that night to a quiet apartment, since her girls were with their father during the summer vacation. She settled into bed for a comfortable sleep.

Due to a late work schedule the next morning, the alarm did not go off until 9:15. Denise opened her eyes—and there in the doorway stood a stranger with his T-shirt pulled up over the bridge of his nose. Only his two fearsome eyes could be seen. In his right hand was a silver revolver.

She rubbed her eyes to make sure this was not a dream. The man began moving forward. "What do you want?" she cried out.

He ordered her to stay where she was on the bed. *Oh, my God!* Denise thought to herself. *Where did he come from? How did he get in here? Jesus, help me! I don't understand....*

Denise continued praying as the man pushed a pillow over her face. *O God, don't let him kill me! I'm alone in a four-story brownstone; everybody else is probably already gone to work. Help me, Lord!*

In the ugly moments that followed, Denise glanced to her right and saw the gun lying on the bed no more than inches from her head. When her attacker finally stood up, he seemed to linger in the room for a while. She managed to remain motionless and quiet. Not even a soft whimper escaped her lips. Eventually she heard his footsteps heading down the hall and out the front door.

Denise sat up, quivering. She called 911, and a squad car soon arrived with a policewoman, who gently guided Denise through the necessary reporting, the trip to the hospital for an examination, and other procedures.

Over the next few weeks Denise understandably decided to move to a new location. She temporarily opted for her mother's vacant house in Bedford-Stuyvesant. It wasn't the safest neighborhood, but at least it was rent-free, and perhaps she could save up for something better in the future.

The next winter proved to be one of our area's coldest in years. Snow piled up and stayed, ice began to penetrate Denise's roof and then leak into the house, and meanwhile, the boiler broke, leaving Denise and her daughters without heat. In the midst of all this, one of the girls contracted chicken pox. What else could possibly go wrong?

For this to happen to anyone is horrendous, but how does a new believer make heads or tails of it? How do you cope and manage to move on?

DAMAGED GOODS

It was soon after her assault, while Denise was still somewhat traumatized and afraid to go out much, that she managed to make it to one of our Sunday services. Choir auditions happened to be announced that day. Denise loved to sing and somehow got the courage to fill out an application, despite her battered and bruised soul.

After passing the vocal test, female applicants are interviewed by Carol for twenty to thirty minutes so she can hear their testimony of faith in Christ, learn more about them, and be sure they want to minister to people rather than just sing music. Denise was the last person Carol interviewed this particular day. She opened up to my wife and shared the horrific, still painful events of the recent past: the rape, the terror, the fear and trauma.

When Carol came home, I sensed she was emotionally spent. She told me about a special choir applicant and her tragic story. "She's a new Christian, Jim, and right now she's 'damaged goods' emotionally. But I sense the Lord wants her in the choir even though she hasn't completely recovered."

I agreed. Carol said I would be meeting her the next evening, when I was scheduled to give a final talk to all the approved applicants.

Denise entered my office with about six other people. As I greeted each with a handshake, she was the only one who avoided eye contact with me. She never looked up once as I spoke for about ten minutes on what the church leadership feels about the choir's potential to bless and serve the congregation. She kept staring at the floor or glancing sideways occasionally. I could feel some of her pain from where I sat, even though I had never seen her before.

When I thanked each of them for their interest in serving the body of Christ, she was expressionless amid all the happiness of the others. I will never forget the sad numbness that enshrouded her that night.

As the choir sang the next Sunday, I searched the alto section for Denise. There she was, properly looking at Carol, singing all the words—with no expression whatsoever. But over time, the Lord began using the other members during practice times, their seasons of prayer, and the Sunday services to lift Denise up from her pain. The challenges of the cold winter and the other difficulties did not disappear overnight. But she began to evidence a new spirit about her.

Months later, as the choir sang a beautiful praise song to the Lord one Sunday night, I began looking again for Denise. There she was in the front row with a joyful radiance on her face, hands lifted high with no self-consciousness whatever. The lady who could not even smile or look at me was gone forever. I wept openly at God's ability to bring her through all kinds of difficulties with victory and joy on the other side.

In time, the tide of bad events began to turn for Denise Tsikudo. One of the men from our church helped her make some repairs on the old house, and an agency called Neighborhood Housing Services gave her a 3 percent loan for a new boiler and weatherproof windows. Another man in the church, who had gone to high school with her, introduced her to his friend Gordon, and a couple of years later they married. A solid Christian home has been built.

"Yes, I went through a lot of stuff that first year," she says. "Through it all, I was just thankful that I had the Lord in my life to help me. What would I have done in similar circumstances without him? I would have given in to my pain and depression.

"The devil wanted me to say, 'Look—I put my faith in Christ, and every time I turn around, something terrible happens. Maybe this wasn't a good idea after all.' But instead, I learned to cling to the Lord. The more troubles that happened, the tighter I had to hold on. And God was faithful."

Not "If," but "When"

Why does God permit trials in our lives? I don't claim to comprehend all of his ways, but we can be sure of these truths:

God uses difficulties and trouble to reveal how deep the Word has gone in our hearts. In the parable of the sower, Jesus told about seed falling in rocky places. "But since they have no root," he said of these plants, "they last only a short time. When *trouble* or *persecution* comes because of the word, they quickly fall away" (Mark 4:17). Notice that Jesus did not say "if" trouble or persecution comes but rather "when" it comes. It is permitted by him as part of our discipline and schooling.

Sometimes we think we're really getting sanctified, we're really growing in the Lord—and then a trial comes along to prove otherwise. Our immature reaction tells us we are not as well rooted as we had assumed.

When the sun is shining and everything is going well, you don't really know what kind of Christian you are. Only the storm reveals that.

In addition to showing our spiritual depth, difficulties have another beneficial effect. Romans 5:3–4 says, "We also rejoice in our sufferings, because we know that suffering produces perseverance; perseverance, character; and character, hope." The way we become people of character is to persevere through hard times. We get through the first difficulty by hanging onto God, and the second one becomes that much more manageable. Eventually we come to resemble a strong tree with deep roots that can stand up to any windstorm.

> Sometimes we think we're really getting sanctified, we're really growing in the Lord—and then a trial comes along to prove otherwise.

Can you actually *rejoice* in suffering? I'm not sure I have reached such a place in God—but I want to get there. Have you ever gotten a phone call from a fellow Christian saying, "Praise God! I just lost my job, and it's wonderful, because it's building character in me—hallelujah!" I haven't lately.

The familiar words of "Amazing Grace" say,

> *Through many dangers, toils and snares*
> *I have already come.*
> *'Twas grace that brought me safe thus far,*
> *And grace will lead me home.*

Carol and the Brooklyn Tabernacle Singers once recorded a simple chorus that says,

> *Hold me, hold me,*
> *I'm in the midst of a storm.*
> *Hold me, hold me,*
> *I'll be safe in my Father's arms.*[1]

I am struck by the honesty of those lyrics. People do go through storms in life, and only God can hold us steady.

Some Christians in certain quarters today have a false sense of dominion as if they are already in heaven, ruling and reigning over the earth with Christ. They think they can create a different reality by saying certain words. That might be a Christian Science teaching, but it's not the Christianity of the Bible. Here on this earth we still have to fight the traffic to the airport, stand in the long lines, squirm in our seat all night, and tug our suitcase down the long corridor and across the busy boulevards—that's all part of the package. But it will be worth it when we get to the beautiful English village.

God is trying to do something more than just give us a smooth life. He is trying to make us like Jesus. He cares more about producing Christlikeness than he does about the American Dream.

Finally, suffering prepares us to serve others in similar predicaments. Paul opens the book of 2 Corinthians by praising "the God of all comfort, who comforts us in all our troubles, so that we can comfort those in any trouble with the comfort we ourselves have received from God. For just as the sufferings of Christ flow over into our lives, so also through Christ our comfort overflows" (1:3–5).

> **God is trying to do something more than just give us a smooth life. He is trying to make us like Jesus.**

God knows that times of trouble are part of the human condition. How else can he raise up an army of anointed comforters in his name unless they have been through the fire themselves? Then, with authority and conviction they can reach out to troubled souls, saying, "I *do* know what you're going through. I've been there myself, and I can tell you that God's grace is sufficient. Hold on—he will bring you through."

BIGGER TARGETS

The devil will try to attack, discourage, and overwhelm any Christian—and especially those with a call to public ministry.

He has a thousand schemes to wear us out, and his ultimate goals are more wicked than we first imagine.

I can still see in my mind the spot in our kitchen where I was sitting when a man of God confronted me with this fact. Our oldest daughter, Chrissy, was at the height of her teenage rebellion, which I wrote about in my first book. My wife, Carol, was still struggling to recover from major surgery. I was at my lowest point. The man stood near the refrigerator and casually said, "You don't think this is really about Chrissy, do you?"

"What do you mean?" I shot back. "Of course it is. That's who we've been interceding for with all our hearts."

"No, it's not just about your daughter," he said. "Do you think the devil just wants her? He wants *you*. He wants your marriage. And more than that, he wants to strike a blow against that church you pastor! So far he hasn't been able to drive a wedge between you and Carol, but he's finding a weak spot in you regarding Chrissy. If he can tear you down and make you act crazy, causing you to 'lose it' and disgrace yourself, the people you pastor will be devastated and vulnerable. That's what he really wants."

At that moment, something rose up in my soul. I knew God was speaking to me through a human instrument. Something inside me said, *God, you're going to hold me! Not only are you going to bring our daughter back to yourself, but you're going to hold me through this trial. Teach me something through all of this mess.*

Praise God that through earnest prayer, the devil's scheme was derailed. I have seen personally how God wonderfully takes what Satan means for evil and turns it for good. I have witnessed that comfort he gives through the storm and have seen it then flow out to others. When Carol and I went through that two-and-a-half year nightmare years ago, I told God in prayer that I would share the testimony of his grace everywhere he sends me. In the years since then, I have done so with many thousands of people in meetings both here and overseas. Many times I have broken down while recounting the heartaches Carol and I went through. But God has used that testimony countless times to stir faith in others. The comfort he gave us has been used to encourage audiences toward fresh strength from God with regard to their own children.

Whatever we may be going through lasts about three seconds compared with eternity. One flash of heavenly glory, and we won't remember the trial at all. In the words of the old gospel song, "It will be worth it all when we see Jesus. . . . One glimpse of his dear face, all sorrow will erase. . . ."

Jesus told his disciples on the last evening just before the powers of darkness began to rage, "In this world *you will have trouble*. But take heart! I have overcome the world" (John 16:33). God does not always take us *out of* difficulty; many times he takes us *through* it. The first shows us God's power, which is omnipotent. The second teaches us the patience, character, and tenderness we need to bless others.

That is another reason why we must return to prayer meetings in the church. They provide a place for us to hold one another up so we don't quit the race. Trials can pull us down if we're alone. When I look out on a Tuesday night and see single moms trying to raise teenagers ... teachers working in the New York City public schools ... men battling the powers of addiction ... I know how desperately we must lift each other up from the muck of life toward the welcoming arms of God.

> **We must return to prayer meetings in the church. They provide a place for us to hold one another up so we don't quit the race.**

On Sundays when broken people come to the front at the end of the message for prayer and help, I will often turn toward the choir and motion for members to come put their arms around these needy souls and guide them to the throne of grace. More than once I have called for Denise, who has responded with love and compassion. The weeping person at the altar has no idea what this woman has been through as she puts her arm around her and begins to pray. Denise has survived the storm herself and therefore ministers with all the more tenderness to the one in need.

God will be faithful to see you through your storm and time of difficulty. Don't look down in discouragement, but look up to him, who has promised to stay with you even "through the valley of the shadow of death" (Psalm 23:4). Did the Lord begin this beautiful work of grace in your life only to let you fall into some black hole of hopelessness and despair? Never! In the end, he will cause you to stand among those

> "... who have come out of the great tribulation; they have washed their robes and made them white in the blood of the Lamb. Therefore,

> "they are before the throne of God
>   and serve him day and night in his temple;
> and he who sits on the throne will spread his tent over
>   them.
> Never again will they hunger;
>   never again will they thirst.
> The sun will not beat upon them,
>   nor any scorching heat.
> For the Lamb at the center of the throne will be their
>   shepherd;
>   he will lead them to springs of living water.
> And God will wipe away every tear from their eyes"
>   (Revelation 7:14–17).

TWELVE

Free Water

O N NEARLY EVERY WEEKLY trip to the supermarket these days, you are sure to be confronted with some new product or packaging. Just when you thought the food companies had done everything imaginable to pique your interest in soda or cheese or popcorn, there's yet another angle, a different flavor, a "new thing under the sun" for you to toss into your cart.

And perhaps the most ingenious is what the marketing gurus have done with the oldest, most basic nourishment of all: water! You thought this was one thing you didn't have to put on your shopping list, because it's freely available from the tap in your kitchen. But no. The brand names on plastic bottles go on for half an aisle, it seems—Aquafina, Calistoga, Evian, Crystal Geyser, Naya, Dasani, Sierra, Deep Rock, Arrowhead, Dannon.... Shoppers are willing to pay real money for some H_2O they believe is just a bit more pure and therefore more healthy.

In the Bible, water is a metaphor for a number of things, but especially a symbol for the person and work of the Holy Spirit. John's gospel records,

> On the last and greatest day of the Feast, Jesus stood and said in a loud voice, "If anyone is thirsty, let him come to me and drink. Whoever believes in me, as the Scripture has said, streams of living water will flow from within him." *By this he meant the Spirit*, whom

those who believed in him were later to receive. Up to that time the Spirit had not yet been given, since Jesus had not yet been glorified (John 7:37–39).

Wherever in the world there is no water, there is no life. People and animals die; vegetation shrivels. In the same way, the Holy Spirit is our only source of spiritual life and energy. This promised "water" keeps us from getting dry and crusty. Whenever we find ourselves becoming arid in our souls, it is due to a lessening influence of the Holy Spirit.

As Samuel Chadwick looked at the needy church climate of his own day, he discerned the real situation: "The remedy . . . is not in reproach and bitterness but in *floods and rivers*, winds and sun. The answer is in the demonstration of a supernatural religion, and the only way to a supernatural religion is in the abiding presence of the Spirit of God."[1]

The same holds true today as we look at the Body of Christ. The problem is not in our lack of buildings, Bible translations, preaching outlines, sound equipment, or financial resources. What we all definitely need is a fresh and abundant supply of the water that brings life.

How much does this wonderful water cost? Is there a spiritual supermarket where God directs us to go and buy it by the gallon? Or can we install a permanent tap and pay for it on a monthly basis? Listen to these truths from the book of Revelation:

> He who was seated on the throne said, "I am making everything new!" Then he said, "Write this down, for these words are trustworthy and true."
> He said to me: "It is done. I am the Alpha and the Omega, the Beginning and the End. To him who is thirsty I will give to drink *without cost* from the spring of the water of life" (Revelation 21:5–6).

"I, Jesus, have sent my angel to give you this testimony for the churches. I am the Root and the Off-
spring of David, and the bright Morning Star."

The Spirit and the bride say, "Come!" And let him
who hears say, "Come!" Whoever is thirsty, let him
come; and whoever wishes, let him take *the free gift* of
the water of life (Revelation 22:16–17).

GOD'S AGENT OF CHANGE

Humanity faces two great spiritual dilemmas. The first is what
to do about our past sins and transgressions, which separate us
from God and produce a guilty conscience. This sense of condemnation makes us shrink from any communion with God—
the very thing for which we were created. But Jesus came and
gave his life so we could be freed from all that. The ugly record
can be erased and our names written in the Book of Life
through the blood that Jesus shed on the cross of Calvary.

But then comes the second problem we all face: How can
we be changed so that we don't go on repeating the same old
sins in the future? How will we rise above the moral pollu-
tion of compulsive sin that caused us to need Jesus in the first
place? Unless Someone can get inside us and overhaul the
very fabric of our being, we will continue to live sinful lives
that grieve God.

God provided a salvation that does more than just forgive our record of past wrongs. He provided victory over
inward sinful desires through the person of the Holy Spirit.
All through this book we have been learning about the abundant life that God intends for his people. We have been seeing the church as it was meant to be. We have been realizing
that only the power of the Holy Spirit can set people free
from their bondage and energize saints for Christian service.

When the Son of God returned to his heavenly throne (Acts 1:9), it ushered in the age of the Holy Spirit. Whatever God is doing today in our world, he is doing through the Holy Spirit. He has no other agent on this planet. We see the incredible start of his working in the book of Acts, and we acknowledge our need to witness the same advances for his kingdom today. So what are the things holding us back?

> **Whatever God is doing today in our world, he is doing through the Holy Spirit. He has no other agent on this planet.**

First of all, some of us apparently are of the opinion that we are basically doing okay in our spiritual life and church life. We don't sense any urgent need for a deeper work by the Holy Spirit. We might not say it in so many words, of course, because it wouldn't sound spiritual. But the truth is, we are not really *thirsty* for the water of the Spirit. There is no sense of discontent, of wanting, of need.

Some with this complacent attitude are afraid of anyone rocking the boat when others begin to hunger and thirst after the living God. Some are even pastors of large, bustling churches that run more on methods and programs than Holy Spirit power. Prayer is negligible or nonexistent, and there is little testimony of the life-changing power of Christ. Members don't live much differently from people in the world, but since the attendance numbers are high, these pastors acquire great influence within their denominations and get quite edgy when thirsty souls begin asking, "Isn't there something more that God has for us?"

But many *are* being stirred by the Spirit of God across our country. They are getting thirsty for the living God to come in blessing and power upon them and their local congregations. There is a deep longing in my own soul for more of the Lord. Only he can satisfy my thirst. Only he can make me the husband, father, pastor, and man of God I need to be. Only he can convict the lost people of Brooklyn and every other city in the world, bringing them to their knees for salvation. Only he can heal the brokenness of this evil world.

I am aware that some people shy away from the Holy Spirit because they have grown up in churches where his name is almost politically incorrect. Instead, the focus has been solely upon the *Word* of God—studying it, dissecting it, memorizing it, comparing one version against another, analyzing the Hebrew and Greek texts, making promises to obey the Bible in all things. . . . Yes, we all must honor and love the Word of God, but there is no getting around the fact that the Bible makes tremendous statements about the Spirit of God! In fact, not only did the Holy Spirit inspire the Scriptures, but he is also ready, willing, and able to fulfill those promises concerning himself.

> **Some people shy away from the Holy Spirit because they have grown up in churches where his name is almost politically incorrect.**

I am well aware that because of the excesses that go on in certain churches—the emotionalism, the psychological manipulations, the wild and zany manifestations—many people have gotten dubious about the Spirit. They watch folks coming week after week for merely emotional fixes, getting "the shakes" or whatever—and then going home to live the same way they have always lived. No spiritual change in them or their churches—no mass water baptisms, no increase in prayer life, no growth in the fruit of the Spirit. Because of this, many sincere believers have said, "No, thank you," and they're right. Unfortunately, they go on to throw out the baby with the bathwater, giving no place at all to the Spirit of God.

Actually, this is a clever tactic of the devil. He uses counterfeit ministers and manifestations to turn people away in fear or distaste. He accents weirdness and unbiblical practices to steer us away from the water we desperately need, so that we find ourselves in a desert of human effort and unbelief.

The fact that there are false gospels in the world does not mean there is not a true gospel. The fact that some parade themselves in the newspaper as a new Jesus or a new messiah does not mean that the true Son of God is not real. And just because some people imitate the moving of the Spirit doesn't mean that God does not have the real thing still available for us today.

Paul spent eighteen months founding a church in Corinth. After he left, false apostles and manipulative charlatans came in and messed up the church to the point that Paul discerned "a different spirit from the one you received" (2 Corinthians 11:4). Satan's counterfeit work is nothing new. He has always tried to distort spiritual things and produce unease about God's power.

I have even been in churches where you almost hesitated to mention the Holy Spirit! You could just feel people tensing up and saying to themselves, *Uh-oh, here comes a roller-coaster ride.* How tragic, and how grievous to the Holy Spirit of God. What hope do we have without his direct personal help?

Now, sincere men and women of God are longing for a return to the New Testament example of the church rather than surrendering to the carnal, prayerless, and powerless models so prevalent today. The religious establishment, of course, will give them the old warnings of "Watch out for that 'Holy Roller business'" or "You don't want that 'deeper life' business."

But the truth is, these thirsty souls don't want any charismatic business, Baptist business, Pentecostal business, or Presbyterian, Nazarene, or Methodist business. They are very interested, however, in some true Holy Spirit business as found in the Scriptures.

TRYING TO PAY

Another roadblock confronting us sounds very spiritual but is in fact the opposite. It has to do with trying to *earn* the refreshing water of the Holy Spirit. Picture in your mind a new Christian—let's call him Alan—who has just come to believe in the Lord Jesus. He has finally realized that he will never be good enough on his own to go to heaven. His good works have not been adequate; he has fallen into sin time and again. Only the grace of the Lord Jesus Christ can settle the moral debts of his past.

A voice in his heart has said, "Alan, you can't earn salvation. It's a gift! Jesus died for you. Reach out your hand and accept his love!" With joy he has received the wonderful gift of eternal life. He knows he doesn't deserve it, but he grate fully accepts it from the hand of a gracious God.

He lives for a while in the euphoria of forgiveness. But very soon, it seems to him that a similar voice is saying, "Alan, you've been reading your Bible, right? There are a lot of things you're not doing for the Lord. You're supposed to love people the way Christ loves them. Are you doing that? You know you're not. You need to try harder, pal. What's wrong with you, anyway?"

Alan starts to fret about his shortcomings. He knows he's impatient at times. On busy days he forgets to have his devotions. At other times he acts in an un-Christlike way. *Oh, God, I'm gonna try harder,* he prays. *You were so kind to save me, and I'm gonna show you I really love you. I'm going to get up earlier in the morning so I can pray more, I really am. I promise to be more of the man you want me to be.*

He keeps his promise for a few days. But by the next Sunday, he is back at the altar confessing his slipups. *God, forgive me—I messed up, but I'm really going to get my act together this week. I know I can do this if I just put my mind to it. I'm really going to try my best. I really promise to be different this time.*

Alan's life settles into a wearisome rhythm of promises, breakdowns, repentance, more promises, more vows, followed by more breakdowns, more confessions . . . until the devil, who comes as an angel of light but is really the great accuser of Christians, whispers, "You know, Alan, you really are a hypocrite. You're not doing what you promised at all. Maybe you ought to just quit the whole race. Why go to church anymore? Why waste your time reading the Bible? You just don't love Jesus enough, and your life shows it."

What is desperately needed in Alan's life is the remembrance of how he started the Christian life in the first place. He didn't earn salvation. He merely opened his hand and received God's free gift.

Can there be a different road now than the one he began? No! Never!

Everything we will ever do or will ever be must come from God, and it comes the same way we started our spiritual walk. As Paul wrote to the Galatians, "Are you so foolish? After beginning with the Spirit, are you now trying to attain your goal by human effort? . . . Does God give you his Spirit and work miracles among you because you observe the law, or because you believe what you heard?" (3:3, 5). In other words, having started with a powerful work of God in our souls, are we now going to live for him on "I promise" power? No, our human effort is totally inadequate for the task. We need the water of the Spirit. God, who began the work in us, must continue it himself.

As one godly writer put it long ago, "All merit is in the Son . . . and all power is of the Spirit." What a profound sentence! The only thing that will ever give you or me acceptance with God is the work of Jesus Christ our Savior. It will never be our own good works. But listen carefully to the corresponding truth: The only power that will keep us victorious on a daily basis comes through the Holy Spirit. It's not about what we can do, but what God can do! His grace does not stop upon our receiving salvation; it is the storehouse from which we draw all we need for the rest of our lives.

What we have in far too many lives today is an Old Testament approach to serving God. We talk about belonging to Jesus but try to please him by obeying the Law in our own self-effort. We are exactly like the Israelites, who told Moses after receiving the Ten Commandments that they would obey everything God said to do. It never worked out that way, for they broke probably all of them within a week. Sincere promises don't cut it; we need outside help from God. If we couldn't forgive our own sin in the first place and had to rely on the shed blood of Jesus, what makes us think we can move ahead subsequently on our own steam?

Just as there is no salvation without Jesus, there can be no Christian living and witness without the Holy Spirit. If you are harboring racist attitudes, it won't help much to only read books and attend sensitivity seminars; God the Holy Spirit must shed his love in your heart. Only then will you stop looking at color and start seeing real people. Black, white, brown—who cares? When the Spirit is controlling you, you don't even notice anymore.

> If we couldn't forgive our own sin in the first place and had to rely on the shed blood of Jesus, what makes us think we can move ahead subsequently on our own steam?

Oh, how we need to wake up to the fact that the Holy Spirit's blessing and power is the key to everything.

And here is the best news: *It's all free!* Salvation is free. The forgiveness of sin is free. A reservation in heaven is free. And the power of the Holy Spirit to live the Christian life is free, too. Everything we need is free from the hand of a gracious God. He waits now to come and meet every need in your life and mine. As the prophet Isaiah proclaimed,

> "Come, all you who are thirsty,
>   come to the waters;
> and you who have no money,
>   come, buy and eat!
> Come, buy wine and milk
>   *without money and without cost*" (55:1).

A BACKWARD APPROACH

When I was a little kid growing up in a legalistic environment, I thought I had to earn the blessing of the Holy Spirit. Somewhere along about the fourth grade, my mother told me I would be less rowdy and stay out of trouble better if I had a deep experience of the Holy Spirit. Some special Monday night prayer meetings were being held in our church, and believe it or not, I actually made it my goal to get onto God's good side at those meetings. I even fasted every Monday for about two months! Imagine a ten-year-old skipping lunch. Surely that would coax God into rewarding me with a Holy Spirit blessing.

It didn't work, however, and in time I realized that God doesn't play the payoff game.

There are sincere speakers and revival movements today that are unconsciously hindering the work of God by saying, "First, overcome the sin in your life; then God will give you the power of his Spirit! When you get victory in your life, then you can come into the place of his full blessing." They have a long list of things that must be done—habits to overcome, devotional practices to establish—all to get you to the place where you can receive the full blessing of Pentecost.

But wait a minute ... how can I overcome my weaknesses, break bad habits, and become more like Christ without the Spirit's power in the first place? If he doesn't help me, I can't move one inch forward in my spiritual life. There is the erroneous suggestion in this teaching that I must move from Point A to Point B in order to "experience the Spirit." The big problem is that I have no ability to get to Point B; only God's grace can get me from Point A all the way to Z.

Such a theology erects hurdles to what God meant as a free gift. In contrast, Jesus simply said, "Are you thirsty? Take a drink of my living water."

But don't things have to change in our behavior? Yes. And God has to make the changes from the inside out. Without God the Holy Spirit working in us, who will change one iota anyway?

For five decades or more, evangelist Billy Graham has wisely concluded his messages with the quiet song "Just as I am, without one plea ... O Lamb of God, I come, I come." He invites his listeners to come for salvation just the way they are.

Any voice that says, *Clean up your act first and then come to Christ*, has to be from Satan. Yes, there must be a turning to God and confession of sin as we place our faith in Christ. But how can I effectively clean up my act without the Holy Spirit's power working within? Forgiveness is free. And so is the Holy Spirit. We can do nothing to merit his presence or

> **Any voice that says,**
> *Clean up your act first and then come to Christ,*
> **has to be from Satan.**

power. We can only come as we are. That is why the apostles used the wording "the *gift* of the Holy Spirit" repeatedly throughout the book of Acts (2:38; 8:20; 10:45; 11:17).

Imagine that my sister, Pat, and her husband, Frank, come over to my house for Christmas, bringing a lovely present for Carol and me. Pat greets me at the front door with a warm hug. "Here, this is for you!" she exclaims as she hands me a large box wrapped in metallic paper and a fancy bow. "Merry Christmas! By the way, that'll be $55, please—cash or check. Either one is fine, but I don't take credit cards."

"Uh, Pat—it's Christmas. What are you talking about? Where's your holiday spirit?"

In other words, if you have to *do something or pay something*, it's not a gift. God simply wants us to freely come, and keep coming, to the fountain that will quench our thirst.

I cling to that phrase in Romans 8:26 again and again: "The Spirit helps us *in our weakness.*" The only qualifications for the fullness of the Spirit are to feel your need, to be thirsty, to want to come to him, pleading your desperate weakness at his throne of grace. *Lord, I am weak. I know that many things in my life really need to change, but I must have your empowerment. I want it to be different in my life, my family, my church, my ministry. But I can't do it in my own strength. Come fill me now with your Holy Spirit.*

Worth the Waiting

The water of God's Spirit is absolutely free, but we must wait by faith continually to receive fresh infillings of this promise from the Father. This is how Luke ends his gospel narrative as he records Jesus' last words to his disciples: "I am going to send you what my Father has promised; but stay in the city until you have been clothed with power from on high" (24:49).

Two thousand years later, this is still the greatest need of the Christian church—to wait regularly in seasons of corporate and individual prayer until we are "clothed with power from on high." These are the *garments* Jesus will still give his people—supernatural ability, might, and power from the Holy Spirit so we can accomplish great things for God's glory.

Think how seldom this promise is preached and emphasized among us—that we can be clothed with the very power of God himself! It is not through human talent or earthly resources that the true Christian church is built, but rather through men and women saturated with God's Spirit and full of his Word.

The word used here for *wait* means literally to "sit still." Jesus knew the disciples' lives would be filled with tremendous amounts of evangelistic and teaching activity, but he commanded them to sit still and wait *first* so God could properly equip them for fruitful ministry. This cycle of waiting on God followed by effective Spirit-filled service is the divine program for all time, not just the New Testament era. Without seasons of prayerful waiting for fresh power, we will see little or no divine assistance in doing God's work. Churches will end up resembling that of Sardis, which the Lord said had "a reputation of being alive, but you are dead" (Revelation 3:1).

Can we not begin to gather across the land in churches and homes to claim this wonderful promise of being "clothed with power from on high"? Why forfeit God's supernatural help, when the signs are all around us that only something from heaven can meet our need? Let pastors begin to lead their congregations in this vital matter of waiting in prayer for God to come and manifest his grace in a greater dimension.

Luke closes his story by relating that the disciples "returned to Jerusalem with great joy and were constantly in the Temple praising and blessing God" (Luke 24:52–53

NKJV). If we put this together with his account in the book of Acts, we see that they went to Jerusalem, visited the temple regularly, and then apparently ended up meeting in the upper room, where the Spirit descended upon them (Acts 2:1–4). The important thing to note is that they went back to the city "with great joy," for they knew that Jesus was risen from the dead! They also knew he would keep his promise of sending them the Holy Spirit's power. Their attitude was not one of morose and depressed introspection but of a joyful looking to God and his faithfulness.

The other important key to their prayerful waiting on God was their regular practice of "praising and blessing God." The meaning of the Greek word for *blessing* here is "to speak highly of, to say great things" about someone. The word for *praising* is used primarily of singing exultation and worshiping God in song.

So there they were: praying, waiting, praising, blessing, singing, and worshiping God with all their hearts. It was not a time of *only* silence, or *only* noise, but rather a joyful mixture of the two, for these Jewish folks knew all too well that God is "enthroned in the praises of Israel" (Psalm 22:3 NKJV). And all this went on *before* the Spirit came in power upon them!

God will act the same way today whenever and wherever his people slow down long enough to give him their total attention in faith-filled prayer, praise, and worshipful waiting. He will transform our lives, invade and bless our churches, and equip us to do things beyond "all we [could] ask or imagine, according to his power that is *at work within us*" (Ephesians 3:20). May fresh power begin this very day to work in and through us as we yield ourselves totally to the Spirit of the living God.

NOTES

Prologue
1. Dwight L. Moody, *Secret Power* (Chicago: Moody, 1881).

Chapter One—A Long Night in Indianapolis
1. Samuel Chadwick, *The Way to Pentecost* (reprint, Dixon, MO: Rare Christian Books, n.d.), p. 19.

Chapter Two—Of Cemeteries and Insane Asylums
1. George Barna, *The Second Coming of the Church* (Nashville: Word, 1998), p. 6.
2. William Law, *The Power of the Spirit* (reprint, Fort Washington, PA: Christian Literature Crusade, 1971), p. 24, italics added.
3. Law, *The Power of the Spirit*, p. 48, italics added.
4. Law, *The Power of the Spirit*, p. 91, italics added.
5. D. Martyn Lloyd-Jones, *The Sovereign Spirit: Discerning His Gifts* (Wheaton, IL: Harold Shaw, 1985), pp. 31, 46.
6. Lloyd-Jones, *The Sovereign Spirit*, p. 25.
7. Charles Haddon Spurgeon, *The Metropolitan Tabernacle Pulpit, 1874*, p. 16: cited in *Spurgeon at His Best* (Grand Rapids: Baker, 1988), p. 102.

Chapter Three—Something from Heaven
1. Cited in V. Raymond Edman, *They Found the Secret* (Grand Rapids: Zondervan, 1960), pp. 83–84.
2. Samuel Chadwick, *The Way to Pentecost* (reprint, Dixon, MO: Rare Christian Books, n.d.), p. 11.
3. Chadwick, *The Way to Pentecost*, p. 13.

Chapter Four—Spirit-Fueled Preaching
1. E. M. Bounds, *Powerful and Prayerful Pulpits* (Grand Rapids: Baker, 1993), p. 43.
2. Andrew A. Bonar, *Heavenly Springs* (Edinburgh: Banner of Truth, 1904), p. 127.

3. Bounds, *Powerful and Prayerful Pulpits*, p. 36.

4. Bounds, *Powerful and Prayerful Pulpits*, p. 34.

Chapter Five—Facing Heat

1. Andrew A. Bonar, *Heavenly Springs* (Edinburgh: Banner of Truth, 1904), p. 19.

2. John Wesley, "Scriptural Christianity," *The Works of John Wesley*, 3d ed., vol. 5 (London: Wesleyan Methodist Book Room, 1872; reprint, Grand Rapids: Baker, 1998), pp. 51–52.

Chapter Six—A House United

1. Paraphrased by David Winter, *100 Days in the Arena* (Wheaton, IL: Harold Shaw, 1977), p. 45.

Chapter Seven—Unqualified?

1. Cited by V. Raymond Edman, *They Found the Secret* (Grand Rapids: Zondervan, 1960), pp. 85–86.

2. Aggie Hurst's autobiography, written with Doug Brendel, is titled *Aggie* (Springfield, MO: Access Publishing, 1986).

Chapter Eight—Getting People Out of Their Prisons

1. Dwight L. Moody, *Secret Power* (Chicago: Moody, 1881), first chapter.

Chapter Nine—Holy Spirit "Strategy"

1. E. Stanley Jones, *Abundant Living* (Nashville: Abingdon Press, 1942), p. 364.

2. Samuel Chadwick, *The Way to Pentecost* (reprint, Dixon, MO: Rare Christian Books, n.d.), p. 15.

3. Cited in J. Paul Reno, *Daniel Nash: Prevailing Prince of Prayer* (Asheville, NC: Revival Literature, 1989), pp. 24–25.

4. L. C. Hall, © 1946 Mrs. L. C. Hall. Assigned 1966 to Gospel Publishing House SESAC.

Chapter Ten—Joy and a Whole Lot More

1. Carol Cymbala, "All That You Need" © 1987 Carol Joy Music. Recorded by the Brooklyn Tabernacle Choir on *Praise Him … Live* (Warner Alliance, 1995).

Chapter Eleven—Through Many Hardships

1. [Still to come.]

Chapter Twelve—Free Water

1. Samuel Chadwick, *The Way to Pentecost* (reprint, Dixon, MO: Rare Christian Books, n.d.), p. 13, italics added.

FRESH POWER
STUDY GUIDE

CHAPTER ONE: A LONG NIGHT IN INDIANAPOLIS

When Pastor Cymbala addressed a large group during a Christian music festival, he said, "God says that when you call, he will answer. The hard cases some of you are facing today—the answer won't come from another seminar.... The answer is not in any human methodology. The answer is in the power of the Holy Spirit. The answer is in the grace of God." Why do you think this is a vitally important message for Christians today?

As recorded in John 16:7, Jesus said to his disciples, "It is for your good that I am going away. Unless I go away, the Counselor [the Holy Spirit] will not come to you; but if I go, I will send him to you." Why did the disciples, who had spent time with Jesus personally, need the Holy Spirit?

A Time to Share

Romans 8:26 reveals, "The Spirit helps us in our weakness. We do not know what we ought to pray for, but the Spirit himself intercedes for us with groans that words cannot express."

- What makes it so difficult for Christians to admit that, on their own, they don't know how to pray and need the Holy Spirit's help?
- What is the danger of relying on how we have learned to pray instead of calling on God to have "the Holy Spirit supernaturally assist us"?
- What are some of the things that keep us, as individual believers or local congregations, from receiving powerful, supernatural assistance from the Holy Spirit so that we, in Pastor Cymbala's words, "can fulfill all of God's will, defeat every device of Satan, and extend the kingdom of Christ here on earth"?

CHAPTER TWO:
OF CEMETERIES AND INSANE ASYLUMS

Why are the following common reactions of the church, pointed out by Pastor Cymbala, so damaging to Christians and non-Christians?

1. "Running away from the world, circling our wagons, and saying, 'Isn't it horrible the way people are living out there?' "
2. "Making harsh and condemning statements about the world and its people, forgetting that they are not our enemy but rather our mission field."
3. "Letting the world 'evangelize' us without our knowing it."

What do you think is the source of the breakdown in the spiritual fiber of some professing Christians that causes them to become more and more like non-Christians? (Be honest!)

When church leaders cover up the church's weaknesses and carnality instead of addressing the lack of prayer, the perceived irrelevance of the Bible, and the reliance on human cleverness, what are some of the consequences?

What is the essential element of a vibrant, spiritually alive church?

Personal Reflection

Pastor Cymbala writes that it is not possible for a Christian to live a "victorious Christian life" without experiencing the Holy Spirit's power. Are you experiencing that power? How are you faring against the evil powers in this world? To what degree are you depending on your own strength rather than on God and his power?

A Time to Share

"There are *no* New Testament verses," writes Pastor Cymbala, "that tell us to dismiss the precedent of the Holy Spirit's activity in Acts."

- What would change—in our lives and our churches— if we believed that the Holy Spirit could accomplish in our lives what he accomplished through simple, untrained men in the early church?
- What is the relationship between the Holy Spirit and the power of God at work in our lives?
- How have false representations of the Holy Spirit's involvement, such as people barking like dogs during church services, affected our view of the Holy Spirit? Our commitment to submit to the authority of Scripture?

- Just as the residents of Berea did many years ago, why is it important for us to "examine" the Scriptures constantly and compare everything to what they say?
- What did Paul mean when he declared in 1 Corinthians 4:6, "Do not go beyond what is written"?

Jesus told his disciples to wait in Jerusalem to "receive power when the Holy Spirit comes on you" (Acts 1:8) because he knew the enemy's power and strongholds. He also knew how much discernment, wisdom, and boldness they would need. What makes it so difficult for us to seek and rely on the Holy Spirit's supernatural power rather than trying to accomplish things on our own?

"The thrust in the New Testament was always toward the power itself rather than any particular manifestations that came alongside the power," Pastor Cymbala writes. What happens when Christians today become fascinated with visible manifestations of the Holy Spirit rather than with the power of the Holy Spirit to do God's work?

Pastor Cymbala tells the story of Michael and Maria, whom God pulled out of drugs and immorality. Today God empowers them to minister to others through Christ Tabernacle in New York City. What is the benefit of hearing real-life examples of how God is changing people's lives through the Holy Spirit's power?

A Time to Share

Jesus said, "You will receive power *when* the Holy Spirit comes on you; and you *will be* my witnesses" (Acts 1:8).

- Is this divine promise still in effect? How do you know?

- What, according to this verse, is the great work of the church?
- What enables us to do this great work?

CHAPTER THREE: SOMETHING FROM HEAVEN

Jesus chose ordinary men—fishermen, a tax collector, a radical Zealot—to be his disciples. "Jesus did this on purpose," writes Pastor Cymbala. "Rather than depending on their human abilities, "they would have to reach out to his promise of 'power from on high.' "

- What can happen to our trust in God's grace as our education, connections, and money increase? Why?
- How do you think the disciples felt as they waited in that upper room in Jerusalem after Jesus' ascension?
- We learn in Acts 2:4 that all of the disciples "were filled with the Holy Spirit." If we believe that the Spirit of God will supernaturally fill and flood ordinary women and men—just like us—and empower us to carry out his will and greatly affect the world around us, what can happen?
- What do our churches need far more than programs, human ideas, talents, and strategies? What is the result when we have it?

Personal Reflection

"The Holy Spirit...," writes Pastor Cymbala, "has come to free us from the restraints and complexes of insufficient talent, intelligence, or upbringing. He intends to do through us what only he can do." Do you believe that God can use anyone who is available and waiting on God—no matter what sins he or she has committed or how many times he or she has failed? What is easier about trusting in your intellect, abilities, and talents than trusting in God and praying daily for the Holy Spirit's power? Where is the source of your strength right now? (Be honest!) How much time are you investing in prayer and waiting upon God so you can be freshly filled with his power?

What are the key differences between teaching and preaching about the Spirit and experiencing him personally? How do those differences relate to the fruitfulness of our service for God?

What does Pastor Cymbala mean when he writes, "We must balance all our activities *for* him [God] with time spent *with* him, waiting in expectant prayer and worship"?

Personal Reflection

How do you find the balance between your human efforts and your dependence on the Holy Spirit's power?

A Time to Share

- How would you answer Pastor Cymbala's question about what keeps us from humbly "setting our hearts toward God in fervent prayer that he will come and revive his work in us as well as in our churches"?
- Why are we so often willing to postpone asking God to give us the divine power we need in order for God to really work in and through us?
- What happens when we absorb, through personal experience in a religious environment, definitions and mental pictures of words such as *worship, prayer, evangelism,* or *preaching* that have not come from prayer-

fully searching God's Word and seeking him with open minds and hearts?

CHAPTER FOUR: SPIRIT-FUELED PREACHING

Do you agree with Pastor Cymbala that in a church "there should always be the element of supernatural assistance that is unexplainable to the natural mind" and that the church should be a "place of awe and wonder"? Why or why not? What differences would you see between such a church and other churches?

A Time to Share

- What did you think as you read Pastor Cymbala's contrasting of New Testament teaching concerning the Holy Spirit's power with today's "user-friendly" approaches that dilute the Bible's message and strive to give attendees what they want to hear?
- How do these words from Paul differ from what you have seen in some churches today? "My message and my preaching were not with wise and persuasive words, but with a demonstration of the Spirit's power, so that your faith might not rest on men's wisdom, but on God's power" (1 Corinthians 2:1–5).
- In what way(s) can we invite the Holy Spirit into our meetings and count on his ministry among us?

Discuss the following points that Pastor Cymbala says comprise the only thing that will satisfy our souls' thirst.

1. "The Holy Spirit's power is our greatest need."
2. "This power and blessing is freely promised to all of God's people."

3. "This promise can only be fully received through sincere praying in faith and through waiting on God for his blessing to come."

Personal Reflection

What may be keeping you from believing what God wants for *you*—no matter what your background may be—and from receiving the power he wants to give you to do his will? Are you willing to take God up on his promises to supply you with the Spirit abundantly and use you in his service as you remain open and obedient to the sovereign mind and moving of the Spirit? Do you believe that the gospel of Christ, through the power of the Holy Spirit, can transform the lives of people you love who seem to be beyond rescue?

Willie McLean didn't seem like someone who would ever find Jesus, but he did—through the power of the Holy Spirit in a church service. Why are the Word *and* the Holy Spirit such a vital combination?

CHAPTER FIVE: FACING HEAT

If spending time in communion with God is so critical to experiencing the Holy Spirit's power, why don't we spend more time praying, reading the Word, and asking God to give us supernatural leadings and other evidences of his power?

Peter, as Pastor Cymbala pointed out, didn't declare healing for every beggar at that temple gate—only one in particular. (See Acts 3.) What does this reveal about how any God-given spiritual gift is to be used?

Why are nonbelievers attracted to Jesus when the Holy Spirit's power is manifested through believers?

A Time to Share

- What is at stake when pastors speak about what people *want* to hear instead of speaking about what they *need* to hear? What difference does it make when a pastor does God's work in God's way by preaching his Word under his power for his glory?
- In Acts 4:8, we read, "Then Peter, filled with the Holy Spirit, said to them...." If Peter was categorically and permanently filled with the Spirit back in the upper room, as some people believe, why do you think this filling is mentioned here?
- What does Paul mean when he says, "God did not give us a spirit of timidity, but a spirit of power, of love and of self-discipline" (2 Timothy 1:7)?
- Pastor Cymbala writes, "We need living arguments, trophies of God's grace, to refute our critics." What might happen—in our lives, in our churches, among non-Christians—if we began to see and hear more clear examples of the miraculous power of God at work in our midst?
- Read Psalm 63:1–5 aloud and discuss, verse by verse, what the psalmist shared and how these verses relate to our lives.

Personal Reflection

- "We can rest assured today," writes Pastor Cymbala, "that whatever God *calls* us to do, he will also be faithful to *equip* us to do." What may God be calling you to do? How are you responding? Why do you need God's equipping in order to pursue his calling?
- When times are difficult, do you cry out in desperation to God? Why or why not? Do you join with

other people in prayer during your time of need? (See Hebrews 4:16.)

Pastor Cymbala points out that each of us needs continual infillings of the Holy Spirit in order to counter the strong, ungodly tendencies of our age. We need "deeper enduements of power" from God in order to meet deeper challenges. So why do we hesitate to entreat God to provide what we need in order to live for him?

CHAPTER SIX: A HOUSE UNITED

Why is it important for us to read and understand this verse as we think about unity: "A new *command* I give you: Love one another. As I have loved you, so you *must* love one another" (John 13:34)?

What has happened to the body of Christ as a result of denominational barriers, divided church boards, and congregational division? What is causing the disunity and division that prevail among some Christians today and are holding back the work of God?

What results when we overlook the actions of people who create division between Christians by gossip or other means and fail to discipline them?

Pastor Cymbala points out that on Sundays in the United States, people of different races usually split up and worship God with people of their own color and ethnic backgrounds— even though "God does not show favoritism" (Acts 10:34). What's at the root of this racial separation? What can we do about it—individually and corporately?

CHAPTER SEVEN: UNQUALIFIED?

Compare the qualifications required for the deacons in the early church ("known to be full of the Spirit and wisdom") with the qualifications often required of similar positions today. In what ways have educational degrees, money, and other factors influenced how church leaders are chosen?

A Time to Share

The Holy Spirit, as Pastor Cymbala emphasizes, is *resident* in every believer born again into salvation. But the New Testament reveals that to be *full* of the Holy Spirit is something distinct and observable—to "keep on being filled with the Spirit" (literal rendition of Ephesians 5:18).

- Why is this a critically important distinction to recognize, and what does it mean to us today?
- Why do you think the term *Spirit-filled* is not often used in many Christian circles today?
- What might the consequences be if the church remembers that God does not work by titles or human resources but by divine gifting, and that even "ordinary" people may overflow with the Spirit of God?

Some people today claim that if we are right with God, repeat his promises, and take authority over every problem, everything in our lives will be great. In what ways does what happened to Stephen, a deacon in the early church, contradict those claims?

Personal Reflection

Pastor Cymbala writes about how God used the sacrifice of David and Svea Flood to lead many Africans to Christ. Which sacrifice(s) have you or someone you know made for the cause of Christ? Do you deem those sacrifices to be worth the price? Why is it that we often minimize what it seems God has done and is doing in and through us rather than trusting that God is accomplishing his will in the spiritual realm? Why is *how* you live more important than *how long* you live? Have you asked God to melt your heart and soften your will so you can be a doer, not just a hearer, of his Word?

Contrast what many people live for, such as wealth or fame, to the challenge God gives us to live for something far greater than ourselves.

CHAPTER EIGHT:
GETTING PEOPLE OUT OF THEIR PRISONS

Do you agree with Pastor Cymbala that "we have developed a religious industry whose machinery runs smoothly without any need of the Holy Spirit"? Why or why not? What are the consequences of this kind of industry?

"Revival," writes Pastor Cymbala, "comes when people get dissatisfied with what is and yearn deeply for *what could be*." He also quotes Luke 11:13: "If you then, though you are evil, know how to give good gifts to your children, how much more will your Father in heaven give the Holy Spirit to those who ask him!" What would you like to see happen in your community? Which steps are you willing to take to bring your needs to God in prayer so his hand will move on your behalf?

Believers in the early church prayed for Peter's release from prison, and God freed Peter from all obstacles just in time.

Why is it often so difficult to keep trusting God to do his work as deadlines near?

CHAPTER NINE: HOLY SPIRIT "STRATEGY"

A Time to Share

- Why do we need the Holy Spirit's leading in daily life?
- What happens to Christians who "sit on the sidelines" and refuse to be champions for God in the struggle against evil?
- In what way(s) does our busyness greatly limit our ability to listen to God so he can tell us specifically what we need to hear?
- What tends to happen when we don't pray and ask God for his direction?
- "I am not interested in debating *how* the Holy Spirit speaks," writes Pastor Cymbala. "He certainly uses more than one way. I want to stay focused on the fact that the Spirit is alive, not dead, and that he *does* speak." How can we distinguish between the Holy Spirit's true speaking, on one hand, and the phonies and frauds who try to move us away from the Spirit's genuine working?

"Gospel work in our day must be more than just little stories, doctrinal presentations, and polite lectures," writes Pastor Cymbala. "It must carry a sense of God's living power. It must show a living Holy Spirit who is still active on the earth." Why is the Holy Spirit's activity so important for us to see and share with other people?

CHAPTER TEN: JOY AND A WHOLE LOT MORE

Jesus said, "I have come that they may have life, and have it to the full.... Ask and you will receive, and your joy may be complete" (John 10:10; 16:24). Given these promises, why do you think many Christians battle depression and experience joyless living?

What do you think is the difference between encouraging people to continue "in the grace of God" (see Acts 13:43) and asking them to make a series of promises and commitments to "live right" in their own strength?

A Time to Share

Philippians 2:13 reads, "It is God who works in you to will and to act according to his good purpose."

- What does this verse reveal about God's grace?
- Which verbs in this verse help us recognize where we need God's help in order to walk in his ways?
- Why is this verse's theme so different from verses related to "Old Testament Christianity" that was based on sinful people's external ability to keep God's holy commands?
- Hebrews 8:7–10 describes God's new covenant with his people. At the end, God said, "I will put my laws *in their minds* and write them *on their hearts*." How is the Holy Spirit's work *within us* different from what we try to do on our own?

- Contrast the following quotation from Pastor Cymbala with the belief that the Holy Spirit's power is an *option* for those of us who desperately want to be like Christ: "The power to be different comes from heaven, not from our own strength. The Holy Spirit was given, as his name implies, so that we can live a holy life for God."

What are some Christians relying on when they try hard to be good and obey God's commands instead of relying on the Holy Spirit continually?

Why, as Pastor Cymbala emphasizes, does the gospel message always attract opposition and rejection when it is presented boldly without pandering to the wishes and preferences of audiences?

The new Christians in ancient Antioch faced trying times after Paul and Barnabas were kicked out of town. Yet "they were more and more filled with joy and with the Holy Spirit" (Acts 13:52). What enabled them to experience joy rather than discouragement?

Where, according to Galatians 5:22–23 and Nehemiah 8:10, does joy come from? How is it produced?

Pastor Cymbala writes about Robin Giles, whose early life was filled with abuse, self-doubt, depression, and anger. Yet God set her free and took the sting out of her past. What does her story reveal about the Holy Spirit's power to transform even the most troubled lives and produce something beautiful?

Chapter Eleven: Through Many Hardships

A Time to Share

Many Christians today, especially in America, have been taught that the Christian life is a smooth ride from the time they accept Christ until they get to heaven.

- What kinds of things happened to the apostle Paul, and what did he say about hardships? (Read Acts 14:1–7, 19–22.)
- How do you respond when you hear Christians preaching that when we learn to make God's promises work for us we will have wonderful lives—money, no trials, no suffering?
- As you think about the verses you read in *Fresh Power* concerning the trouble Christians will face (Job 5:7; Acts 14:19–22; 1 Thessalonians 3:2–4; 2 Timothy 3:10–12), how should Christians respond when "stuff" happens to them or to someone they love?
- Do you agree with Pastor Cymbala that it is a "terrible deception" to tell people that once they become Christians they will live on "spiritual Easy Street" rather than telling them the full scope of God's truth? Why or why not?
- What are the dangers of picking and choosing favorite verses and ignoring other verses with which we don't agree?

Personal Reflection

Why is it important for Christians to realize that the Christian life is not free of troubles? What are some of the consequences when Christians aren't willing to admit that trials will come in their lives? What happens when Christians overlook that truth during discussions with non-Christians?

As Pastor Cymbala points out, the Greek word the apostle Paul used (Acts 14:19–22) that is "translated 'hardships' means to break, crush, compress, squeeze. It signifies distress, pressure, a burden upon the spirit." When you face hardships in your life, in spite of all the prayer and support you may be receiving, how do you respond? When you read in 1 Thessalonians 3:3 that Christians are "destined" for trials, how do you feel?

Why is it so important for us to correctly handle the word of truth (2 Timothy 2:15)—to interpret Scripture faithfully and accurately?

"I am finding out that in Christian conferences and meetings today," writes Pastor Cymbala, "not everyone is open to the Word of God. Many have their own agendas and traditions, which they dearly cherish even though they contradict or deny Scripture." Why are such people so concerned about maintaining the status quo and resistant to any hint that God desires to change some part of their lives or church ministries? What are the dangers?

What might happen if more Christians embraced scriptural principles and refused to be satisfied with compromise and unbelief?

"When the sun is shining and everything is going well," Pastor Cymbala writes, "you don't really know what kind of Christian you are. Only the storm reveals that." What do the storms we face reveal and teach us—about ourselves, about God, about how God is shaping us, about our sense of security, about what it means to serve and comfort others?

Pastor Cymbala describes the Tuesday evening prayer meetings at the Brooklyn Tabernacle when people "lift each other up from the muck of life toward the welcoming arms of God." Why are such prayer meetings so necessary today?

Personal Reflection

When you face storms and difficulties, do you believe that God will remain faithful? Would you say that you "look down in discouragement" or "up" to God? Think carefully about your answers and what God may be trying to teach you through difficult times.

CHAPTER TWELVE: FREE WATER

"Not only did the Holy Spirit inspire the Scriptures," writes Pastor Cymbala, "but he is also ready, willing, and able to fulfill those promises concerning himself" in the Bible. How much do you long for more of the Lord, who alone can satisfy your spiritual thirst? How strong is your commitment to him—and to acknowledging your need for the Holy Spirit's work in your life? In which areas of your life do you urgently need the Holy Spirit's working?

A Time to Share

According to Pastor Cymbala, what the body of Christ needs is "a fresh and abundant supply of the water that brings life"— the Holy Spirit. It is a free gift to us from God that provides victory over our inward sinful desires. Yet many of us try to "fix ourselves" rather than to depend on the power of the Holy Spirit to set us free. Discuss how each of the following limits, or damages, the Holy Spirit's work in our lives.

- Our belief that we are doing okay in our spiritual life and church life and don't have an urgent need for the Holy Spirit.
- We shy away from asking what more God may have for us because we don't want to rock the boat and risk changing the status quo.
- We have grown up in churches that focus solely on teaching the Word of God and shy away from the Holy Spirit.
- We are dubious about the Holy Spirit, having heard or even seen the excesses that go on in certain churches—emotionalism, psychological manipulations, wild manifestations, etc.
- Our inability to recognize counterfeit ministers and manifestations that turn people away from the Holy Spirit, whom we desperately need.
- Our desire to *earn* the refreshing water of the Holy Spirit by trying to do the right things by human effort.

In Galatians 3:3, 5, Paul writes, "Are you so foolish? After beginning with the Spirit, are you now trying to attain your goal by human effort?... Does God give you his Spirit and work miracles among you because you observe the law, or because you believe what you heard?" What do these verses reveal about trying to live for God in our human effort, about trying to please Jesus and overcome our sin without relying on outside blessing and power from God's Spirit?

Why do you think the apostles used the wording the "*gift* of the Holy Spirit" repeatedly throughout the book of Acts? (See 2:38; 8:20; 10:45; 11:17.) What does that usage communicate to you?

What do you think this phrase from Romans 8:26 means: "The Spirit helps us in our weakness"? Why would this help be important?

In his prayer for the Ephesians, Paul writes, "Now to him who is able to do immeasurably more than all we ask or imagine, according to his power that is at work within us" (Ephesians 3:20). How can we encourage one another to give God our total attention and ask him to do this in our lives and in our churches?

Personal Reflection

Pastor Cymbala writes, "The water of God's Spirit is absolutely free, but we must wait by faith continually to receive fresh infillings" of the Holy Spirit, to be "clothed with power from on high" (Luke 24:49). What may be keeping you from prayerfully waiting for fresh power from God? What difference would more of God's supernatural power make in your life and in the lives of people around you? What steps will you take during the coming days to slow down long enough to give God your total attention in faith-filled prayer, praise, and worshipful waiting?